CONTENTS

PREFACE   1
Catherine M. Wehlburg

1. Integrated General Education: A Brief Look Back   3
Catherine M. Wehlburg
This chapter is an overview of historical trends that have taken general education from the concept of a unified curriculum with no distinction between "specialized" and "general" education to the current distribution requirement that many institutions use.

2. Since We Seem to Agree, Why Are the Outcomes So Difficult to Achieve?   13
Terry Rhodes
The Valid Assessment of Learning in Undergraduate Education (VALUE) project is described and results are presented, along with assessment of outcomes positioned in a national and international context.

3. Making General Education Matter: Structures and Strategies   23
Joan Hawthorne, Anne Kelsch, Tom Steen
This chapter focuses on the process used by the University of North Dakota to engage faculty in general education reform by making the program matter to faculty across disciplines. Their process resulted in a new program that is engaging much of the campus community in creation of a vertically integrated general education program.

4. Unifying the Undergraduate Curriculum Through Inquiry-Guided Learning   35
Virginia S. Lee, Sarah Ash
This chapter discusses development of a framework for integrating undergraduate curriculum across general education and the major. Participating faculty and staff members agreed on four overarching intended learning outcomes as the distinctive feature of inquiry-guided learning: critical thinking, habits of independent inquiry, taking responsibility for one's own learning, and intellectual growth and maturity.

5. University of the Pacific's Bookend Seminars on a Good Society   47
Lou Matz
The signature component of the University of the Pacific's general education program is three required Pacific Seminars (PACS) that focus on the question, "What is a Good Society?"

6. Core Curriculum Revision at TCU: How Faculty Created 59
and Are Maintaining the TCU Core Curriculum
Edward McNertney, Blaise Ferrandino
This chapter describes the faculty-led, participatory process of creating
an outcomes-based core curriculum at Texas Christian University.

7. Creating an Integrative General Education: 69
The Bates Experience
Jill Reich, Judy Head
The Bates College general education curriculum is used in this chapter
to articulate the importance of several integrative goals and processes
that make up our new General Education curriculum.

8. Building an Integrated Student Learning Outcomes 79
Assessment for General Education: Three Case Studies
Jo K. Galle, Jeffery Galle
Looking across three institutions, the authors found that a three-stage
process for developing an integrated general education assessment plan
allowed for institutional differences. What emerged from their work
demonstrates the remarkable ways in which institutions of various
kinds adapted the stages to fit their own unique academic culture and
necessities.

9. Meaningful General Education Assessment That Is 89
Integrated and Transformative
Catherine M. Wehlburg
This chapter describes a transformative approach to assessing general
education programs, identifies potential obstacles to successful assessment, and outlines necessary steps for creating assessable outcomes-
based programs.

INDEX 99

New Directions for
Teaching and Learning

Marilla D. Svinicki
Catherine M. Wehlburg
CO-EDITORS-IN-CHIEF

Integrated General Education

Catherine M. Wehlburg

EDITOR

Number 121 • Spring 2010
Jossey-Bass
San Francisco

INTEGRATED GENERAL EDUCATION
Catherine M. Wehlburg (ed.)
New Directions for Teaching and Learning, no. 121
Marilla D. Svinicki, Catherine M. Wehlburg, Co-Editors-in-Chief

Microfilm copies of issues and articles are available in 16mm and 35mm, as well as microfiche in 105mm, through University Microfilms, Inc., 300 North Zeeb Road, Ann Arbor, MI 48106-1346.

NEW DIRECTIONS FOR TEACHING AND LEARNING (ISSN 0271-0633, electronic ISSN 1536-0768) is part of The Jossey-Bass Higher and Adult Education Series and is published quarterly by Wiley Subscription Services, Inc., A Wiley Company, at Jossey-Bass, 989 Market Street, San Francisco, CA 94103-1741. Periodicals postage paid at San Francisco, CA, and at additional mailing offices. POSTMASTER: Send address changes to New Directions for Teaching and Learning, Jossey-Bass, 989 Market Street, San Francisco, CA 94103-1741.

New Directions for Teaching and Learning is indexed in CIJE: Current Index to Journals in Education (ERIC), Contents Pages in Education (T&F), Current Abstracts (EBSCO), Educational Research Abstracts Online (T&F), ERIC Database (Education Resources Information Center), Higher Education Abstracts (Claremont Graduate University), and SCOPUS (Elsevier).

SUBSCRIPTIONS cost $98 for individuals and $267 for institutions, agencies, and libraries in the United States. Prices subject to change.

EDITORIAL CORRESPONDENCE should be sent to the co-editor-in-chief, Marilla D. Svinicki, Department of Educational Psychology, University of Texas at Austin, One University Station, D5800, Austin, TX 78712.

www.josseybass.com

FROM THE SERIES EDITORS

About This Publication

Since 1980, *New Directions for Teaching and Learning (NDTL)* has brought a unique blend of theory, research, and practice to leaders in postsecondary education. *NDTL* sourcebooks strive not only for solid substance but also for timeliness, compactness, and accessibility.

The series has four goals: to inform readers about current and future directions in teaching and learning in postsecondary education, to illuminate the context that shapes these new directions, to illustrate these new directions through examples from real settings, and to propose ways in which these new directions can be incorporated into still other settings.

This publication reflects the view that teaching deserves respect as a high form of scholarship. We believe that significant scholarship is conducted not only by researchers who report results of empirical investigations but also by practitioners who share disciplinary reflections about teaching. Contributors to *NDTL* approach questions of teaching and learning as seriously as they approach substantive questions in their own disciplines, and they deal not only with pedagogical issues but also with the intellectual and social context in which these issues arise. Authors deal on the one hand with theory and research and on the other with practice, and they translate from research and theory to practice and back again.

About This Volume

An integrated general education program can have an impact on overall student learning and make for a coherent approach to the baccalaureate degree. This issue of *NDTL* explores several models of integrated general education programs and includes information on some methods for designing useful and meaningful assessment plans for general education.

Marilla D. Svinicki
Catherine M. Wehlburg
Co-Editors-in-Chief

MARILLA D. SVINICKI *is the director of the Center for Teaching Effectiveness at the University of Texas at Austin.*

CATHERINE M. WEHLBURG *is the assistant provost for Institutional Effectiveness at Texas Christian University.*

PREFACE

General education has been an essential part of American higher education for a long time. Unfortunately, it is seen by many students, faculty, and even parents as something to get out of the way so that the student can go on to learn the more "important" courses within a chosen major. This way of thinking does a disservice to the student, the student's learning, and the overall expectations for a baccalaureate degree. Institutions of higher education have a responsibility to develop a meaningful general education curriculum that cultivates the qualities of thinking, communication, and problem solving (to name a few of the general education goals that many institutions share). What is missing from many institutions, though, is the concept of integrating general education with the overall educational curriculum. If this is done, the general education courses are no longer something to quickly take so they can be checked off; instead, they became part of the ongoing educational development of the student. The goals of general education are more than a list of courses from which to choose; these goals (when met) can help to support a student's future.

The topic for this volume addresses a significant area in higher education: how to integrate and assess (meaningfully) a general education curriculum. Several institutions are working toward this goal, and they have shared their experiences here.

Catherine M. Wehlburg
Editor

CATHERINE M. WEHLBURG is the assistant provost for institutional effectiveness at Texas Christian University. She has taught psychology and educational psychology courses for more than a decade, serving as department chair for some of that time and then branching into faculty development and assessment. Wehlburg has worked with both the Higher Learning Commission of the North Central Association and the Commission on Colleges with the Southern Association of Colleges and Schools as an outside evaluator. She earned her Ph.D. in educational psychology from the University of Florida.

NEW DIRECTIONS FOR TEACHING AND LEARNING, no. 121, Spring 2010 © Wiley Periodicals, Inc.
Published online in Wiley InterScience (www.interscience.wiley.com) • DOI: 10.1002/tl.382

1

By tracing the historical roots of general education, we can make many of our current issues and problems in general education more understandable. This chapter is an overview of historical trends that have taken general education from the concept of a unified curriculum with no distinction between "specialized" and "general" education to the current distribution requirement that many institutions use.

Integrated General Education: A Brief Look Back

Catherine M. Wehlburg

The Association of American Colleges and Universities (AAC&U) has defined general education to be "the part of a liberal education curriculum shared by all students. It provides broad exposure to multiple disciplines and forms the basis for developing important intellectual and civic capacities" (AAC&U, 2009b). General education is therefore an essential and critical piece of the overall undergraduate educational experience. Unfortunately, a majority of faculty and students consider general education requirements to be something to get out of the way so that a student can concentrate on their major courses. This separation of general education from the major and other educational requirements does a disservice to the student and American higher education. General education does not exist in a vacuum. It is a part of every student's baccalaureate education and should be viewed as a method of enhancing the overall level of learning for university graduates.

A Look Back at General Education

The undergraduate educational process did not begin with a specified general education curriculum. Indeed, in early American higher education there was a unified curriculum that focused largely on classical studies. Over time, however, a new emphasis on education as a means to prepare individuals for a variety of vocations caused modifications in how general education has

NEW DIRECTIONS FOR TEACHING AND LEARNING, no. 121, Spring 2010 © Wiley Periodicals, Inc.
Published online in Wiley InterScience (www.interscience.wiley.com) • DOI: 10.1002/tl.383

3

been offered to students. The pendulum has swung back and forth several times between a unified and coherent set of requirements and a wide offering of courses that may result in a disjointed educational experience. But by better understanding the historical causes of the changes in our general education system, we find it clearer that this discussion has certainly been an extended one and will likely continue for many years to come.

Often considered the beginning of American higher education, Harvard University (founded in 1636) initially required college students to take a single curriculum (Boning, 2007). In other words, there was no "general education" that was separate from the "major" program of study that a student was required to take. During this time period, the typical student was a young man who took a specific program of study to go into the church, law, or medicine; there was no need for a student to have options or choices about the coursework he would take (Boyer & Levine, 1981; Boning, 2007). Students took a predetermined set of courses as they prepared for their future, and these courses were decided by the faculty. The set of courses was focused on the classics and was considered appropriate for a young man from a privileged background. This early approach to higher education was coherent because all students took essentially the same courses. Faculty knew what the students knew and what they had taken, and as students graduated from college there was general agreement on what they knew because they had all been educated by taking the same coursework.

When Charles Eliot was inaugurated as the president of Harvard University in 1869, he instituted an "elective" system so that students could individualize their undergraduate study (Miller, 1988). The elective system worked well in many ways: students could choose courses that fit their specific interests and needs, departments could grow as more students took courses from a specific area, and the range of the course offerings increased dramatically (Gaff, 1983). But because students could choose their own sequence of general education courses, some problems developed: "Their choices were so varied that students earning the same degree at the same institution may not have taken any of the same courses" (Boning, 2007, p. 5). There was no unification or integration of what it meant to have a baccalaureate degree. The elective system offered many options for students to choose from, and it allowed the faculty to teach courses within their specific discipline (and increase research productivity). Therefore it "enhanced the professor's love of specialization" (Bisesi, 1982, p. 200). During this time, the role of the department became more pronounced and influential. In this same time period, Johns Hopkins University opened (in 1876). Introduction of an institution with a research-oriented graduate school meant faculty specialization and an increase in the overall knowledge base, which augmented the overall number of courses that students could take and that faculty were interested in teaching. Thus, we have what Bisesi (1982) called the "expanding boundaries" of what was considered part of a program in higher education. There were more options for students with regard to disciplines and career choices because there were more knowledge areas. With this longer list of career and course choices, the concept of a unified or general education began to lose its attraction. Students did not want to be educated all in the same way, taking the same courses. There was now a need to be prepared for any number of areas that were developing quickly as knowledge expanded and more career options were cultivated. In addition, the Morrill Land-Grant act of 1862 provided funding for each state to establish at least one college that focused on agriculture and the mechanic arts. Thus the federal government was promoting education to develop education in the agricultural industry. Creation of the land-grant colleges opened up higher education to a wider and more heterogeneous student population (Boning, 2007). By the end of the 1800s, student preparation was focused on advancement of knowledge within a larger number of specific disciplines (Gaff, 1983): "The elective system became nothing more than a means for students to take whatever classes they wanted on their way to a degree, no matter how fragmented and incoherent their experiences were" (Boning, 2007, p. 5).

As overall undergraduate education programs lost their coherence, reform programs were instituted to change the openness of the elective system. The realization that students did not have a common set of courses and thus could not engage in common discourse created graduates whose preparation level and overall capabilities varied widely. In addition, American universities began to admit more students, and many did not have specific career or vocational plans. To meet their needs, colleges would often require that they take introductory courses from several disciplinary areas. In the early 1900s, a distribution structure was created by the successor to Eliot at Harvard, Abbot Lawrence Lowell. In his 1909 inaugural address, Lowell stated, "It is absurd to suppose that a list of electives alone will furnish him with the required knowledge, or that sense of responsibility which always sits lightly upon the undergraduate will inspire him with wisdom in arranging his course of study" (1934, p. 4). Students were required to take courses in the biological sciences, physical sciences, social sciences, and the humanities in order to better coordinate academic experiences in general education (Thomas, 1962). This idea attracted the attention of many other institutions, and distribution requirements were instituted widely (Cohen, 1988). The distribution requirements still allowed some choice in selecting courses, but they decreased the overall flexibility of an open elective system. By requiring some type of a common curriculum, in addition to disciplinary specificity, this distribution requirement was distinctively different from the earlier subject-centered focus. Thus the general education movement was begun.

Once the concept of general education became more accepted, the forms of implementation began to vary widely. Some of this was based on the specific needs of the society, and on what were considered to be important subjects for all students to study, regardless of disciplinary choice.

As World War I began, a faculty member from the Massachusetts Institute of Technology was asked by the U.S. War department to create a course, later called War Issues. This course was important in the history of general education reform because it focused on a particular contemporary social issue and was created as a direct reaction to current events rather than being from a specific discipline. Following the war, it was transformed into a Contemporary Civilizations course by Columbia University and is still a requirement for their students (Bisesi, 1982).

But not all forms of a general education model were focused on contemporary issues. The University of Chicago created a four-year structure (including the last two years of high school and the first two years of college) that focused on four main areas: biological science, physical science, social science, and the humanities. The purpose of this was to present content essential to all students, regardless of their chosen discipline of study. This program was the basis for what later became the Great Books curriculum that is still used in many institutions. Amherst University, led by Alexander Meiklejohn, wanted an integrated approach that "relied on classical ideas and themes to facilitate problem-solving skills" (Boning, 2007, p. 7). This creation of an interdisciplinary and thematic program resulted in an experimental college that was later developed at the University of Wisconsin. Thus, in the years preceding World War II the rise of general education was in reaction to the previous freedom of the elective system. There was a belief that overspecialization had occurred and students were not receiving a coherent and integrated education.

The 1945 Harvard report "General Education in a Free Society" (often called the "Red Book") proposed the need for both a coherent general education program and a specialized, disciplinary curriculum. This report suggested that general education should be one-third of the overall baccalaureate program so that students did not overspecialize in a single content area. A core curriculum for Harvard University would, according to the report, increase the integration and coherence of the overall education of its students. The report stated that "we are living in an age of specialization, in which the avenue to success often lies in [the student's] choice of a specialized career . . . yet we must envisage the fact that a society controlled wholly by specialists is not a wisely ordered society. . . . The problem is how to save general education and its values within a system where specialism is necessary" (Harvard University, 1945, p. 53). Although Harvard University did not approve this proposal, the report had an impact on general education programs for many years. However, there were difficulties in implementing this type of coherent, interdisciplinary program: "It seemed that general education programs succeeded when departments and disciplines cooperated, but the power of the departments was such that few faculty would attempt interdisciplinary courses when their evaluations and promotions were usually based on work done within the discipline" (Bisesi, 1982, p. 205). The tension between the need for an interdisciplinary, integrated

NEW DIRECTIONS FOR TEACHING AND LEARNING • DOI: 10.1002/tl

general education program and the need for specialization within the discipline made it difficult to find consensus on an overall educational path for students to take. Faculty time, reward structures, and interest in general education are all themes that still exist in the twenty-first century.

In the 1960s, complex social changes and legal decisions affected American higher education. The Higher Education Act of 1965 was passed, which increased federal funding to universities and created scholarships and low-interest loans for students. The result of this was greater diversity, and higher education became more accessible to a wider range of students, including more women and students from underrepresented populations. Students reacted to the general education programs and insisted that it reflect the perspectives of all students and become a more useful preparation for a vocation (Gaff, 1983; Boning, 2007): "By and large, the only impact of student uprisings at Berkeley was the reduction of general education requirements and the minimizing of faculty constraints" (Bisesi, 1982, p. 207). Between 1967 and 1974 almost three-quarters of all universities reduced their general education requirements (Boning, 2007) and increased the number of electives students could take. In general, faculty were able to better focus on their own area of specialization because the need to teach courses within the general education program had lessened. Senior faculty often chose to teach in their specific disciplinary area because of interest and the faculty reward structure. This left the teaching of interdisciplinary and general education courses to the nontenured or tenure-track faculty. Teaching within the major clearly was the way to tenure and promotion at most institutions. Faculty became more committed to their discipline and department than to their institution. In his 1970 address to the Association of American Colleges, Edward Shoben stated that "faculty members widely commit their primary allegiance to their domain of study rather than to an institution and its students" (p. 28). During this period, specialization increased again and the coherence and integration of general education programs was further diminished.

In 1977, a report by the Carnegie Foundation for the Advancement of Teaching, "Missions of the College Curriculum," was published. It decried the state of general education, calling it a "disaster area" and blaming the incoherence of general education programs for devaluation of the baccalaureate degree (p. 11). Ernest Boyer wrote that "electives, with their emphasis on individual interests, continue to increase while general education is in shambles. . . . We are more confident about the length of education than we are about its substance" (1982, p. 582). Thus begins what Boning calls the "third era" in educational reform (2007). During this time period, many types of general education programs were developed. Some are reminiscent of programs used in the past, while others are hybrid models that take into consideration the needs and culture of the individual institution. Most institutions developed a general education curriculum that uses a distribution model in whole or in part. According to a survey of members of AAC&U

(2009a), 80 percent use some type of distribution requirement in their general education program. However, only 15 percent use that model alone. The remaining institutions use some combination of distribution models with common intellectual experiences, thematic courses, or a core curriculum where all students take the same set of courses.

A Look at the Current State of Affairs

Clearly, the pendulum has swung back and forth from a more formalized general education to an open, wider selection of courses several times. But according to Gaff (2003), there has been a more constant focus on general education at most institutions in recent years. Why would this be the case? What is it about the current time that is causing this to happen? One possible reason is that accreditation requirements mandate that general education programs have specified outcomes and appropriate assessment plans in place. This requires that institutions come to agreement about the purpose and goals of their own specific general education programs. Thus general education programs are scrutinized more carefully by accreditation visiting teams. A second possibility is that many institutions have created new positions for leadership of their general education program: "Individuals specifically assigned to provide leadership for general education have a responsibility to keep it vital" (Gaff, 2003, p. 31). Finally, a great deal more is now publicly shared about general education programs than ever before. There are conferences, journals, and books, all focused on general education. The pendulum may not have stopped swinging, but there are clearly important issues that need further discussion, research, and time if we are to determine what the next era in general education reform may be.

Current Issues in General Education

If, as Boning indicates, we are now in the third era of general education reform, there are several overarching themes that are demonstrated in current general education programs. Several are outlined in subsequent chapters as well. But these issues are important here because they can help to guide creation of models for general education that meet the specific needs of individual institutions and their students.

Student learning outcomes for general education are now required by all regional accreditors in the United States. As a result of this mandate, institutions have had to create or at least identify the goals of their programs and determine how they will be measured. Given the often interdisciplinary nature of many general education programs, this has proved to be quite difficult. Trying to measure critical thinking or problem solving across a curriculum can be daunting. The balance between ensuring that general education goals and outcomes are sufficiently broad for an entire institution and yet also specifically measurable is indeed a challenge. Although there are several methods and models to use in designing and implementing an assessment plan for general education (see Chapter Nine for more information), this remains a difficult issue.

First Year Experience (FYE) programs are often connected with general education. According to the AAC&U's recent survey (2009a), 58 percent of its member institutions had FYE programs as part of general education. Although FYE programs have many goals, most focus on introducing the first-year student to the institution, preparing them for university-level education, and affording some element of general education (global understanding, cultural awareness, or ethical thinking). Because FYE programs are often requirements of general education, they can become pathways to communicate expectations to students and ensure that there is a common baccalaureate experience.

Interdisciplinary areas of study have long been a component of general education. Indeed, 51 percent of AAC&U's member institutions include interdisciplinary courses in their general education program (2009a). This is such a broad category, however, that it is difficult to make comparisons across institutions. Some institutions have specific courses that are interdisciplinary, while others have entire programs that are inquiry-based or thematic. Elements of institutional goals for general education often lend themselves well to an interdisciplinary focus—social responsibility, for example, is a topic that can be reflected across many disciplines.

General education requirements that have a diversity or multicultural focus are more common. Fifty-six percent of AAC&U member institutions indicate that diversity studies are a part of their general education program (2009). Some diversity courses are more of a "token" nod to real multicultural education, but there are many general education programs that include transformative experiences for students (Adams & Jay, 2007). This appears to be a growing area and one that will continue to be an issue in general education.

Service learning activities are often part of general education programs because of the pedagogy used rather than the content taught. This teaching method blends an academic classroom experience with some type of meaningful service within the community. More than volunteer work, students in courses with a service learning component learn from their experience and give service to the community. As the goals of general education continue to move in the direction of civic responsibility and social understanding, this type of pedagogy will become more prevalent. There are difficulties in using this technique, however. It can take a great deal of faculty time, before the course even gets under way, to set up an appropriate relationship with a community partner. But there are benefits in that students can gain experiences and demonstrate learning authentically. Thirty-eight percent of AAC&U member institutions report that they include service learning in their general education program (2009a), and this number appears to be increasing.

Integrated General Education

General education is a modern conceptualization of an old idea. But integrating this concept with the overall educational curriculum has the potential to transform how students view their baccalaureate experience. As the twenty-first century begins, many institutions have two programs that students are required to take: at least one major and a general education curriculum. General education courses are often seen as something to get out of the way so that students can take the courses they really came to the institution for; or, these courses are viewed as a way to take several courses in an effort to find an interesting major. In either case, the general education curriculum is rarely seen as something important, worthwhile, and essential to a student's overall education.

However, by integrating the general education experience with the major course work, it is possible to create a new and better understanding of the undergraduate education experience. With appropriate rigor, incorporation of both areas can enhance one another. Transfer of learning may occur more easily; students may be able to bring critical-thinking or problem-solving skills gained from their general education core into their major courses. Content from the major may influence how a student views information in the general education courses. With integration, students might be better prepared for diverse and unexpected requirements in future careers. A coherent educational program that combines all of a student's educational experiences might increase retention and overall learning. The possibilities of revitalizing curriculum by instituting an integrated general education are almost endless. In the following chapters, several models of an integrated general education curriculum are presented. These are just some of the exciting curricular designs that are occurring at many institutions.

References

AAC&U (2009a). Trends and emerging practices in general education. Retrieved October 1, 2008, from http://www.aacu.org/membership/documents/2009Member Survey_Part2.pdf.

AAC&U. (2009b). *What is a liberal education?* Retrieved October 1, 2008, from http://www.aacu.org/leap/what_is_liberal_education.cfm.

Adams, S., & Jay, G. (2007). Service learning, multicultural education, and the core curriculum: A model for institutional change. *Diversity Digest, 10*(2), 9–11.

Bisesi, M. (1982). Historical developments in American undergraduate education: General education and the core curriculum. *British Journal of Educational Studies, 30*(2), 199–212.

Boning, K. (2007). Coherence in general education: A historical look. *Journal of General Education, 56*(1), 1–16.

Boyer, E. L. (1982). Seeing the connectedness of things. *Educational Leadership, 39*(8), 582–584.

Boyer, E. L., & Levine, A. (1981). *A quest for common learning: The aims of general education.* Washington, DC: Carnegie Foundation for the Advancement of Learning.

Carnegie Foundation for the Advancement of Teaching. (1977). *Missions of the college curriculum: A contemporary review with suggestions.* San Francisco: Jossey-Bass.

Cohen, A. M. (1988). *The shaping of American higher education: Emergence and growth of the contemporary system.* San Francisco: Jossey-Bass.

Gaff, J. G. (1983). *General education today: A critical analysis of controversies, practices, and reforms.* San Francisco: Jossey-Bass.

Gaff, J. G. (2003). Keeping general education vital: A struggle against original sin? *Peer Review, 5*(1), 31.

Harvard University, Committee on the Objectives of a General Education in a Free Society. (1945). *General education in a free society: Report of the Harvard Committee.* Cambridge: Harvard University Press.

Lowell, A. L. (1934). *At war with academic traditions in America.* Cambridge, MA: Harvard University Press.

Miller, G. E. (1988). *The meaning of general education: The emergence of a curriculum paradigm.* New York: Teachers College Press.

Shoben, E. (1970). The liberal arts and contemporary society: The 1970s. *Liberal Education, 56*(1), 28–38.

Thomas, R. (1962). The search for a common learning: General education, 1800–1960. New York: McGraw-Hill.

CATHERINE M. WEHLBURG is the assistant provost for institutional effectiveness at Texas Christian University. She has taught psychology and educational psychology courses for more than a decade, serving as department chair for some of that time and then branching into faculty development and assessment. Wehlburg has worked with both the Higher Learning Commission of the North Central Association and the Commission on Colleges with the Southern Association of Colleges and Schools as an outside evaluator. She earned her Ph.D. in educational psychology from the University of Florida.

2

There is mounting evidence from faculty and employers that a broad set of skills and abilities are essential for student success as graduates, citizens, and employees. The traditional approach to general education with an emphasis on exposure to a menu of knowledge no longer suffices. Graduates need to be able to integrate their learning, apply it in real-world settings, and use it to address complex and unscripted problems. Examining the emergent research on student learning and key factors that deepen and enhance learning in essential areas for all students at our institutions leads us to developing new modes of measuring and assessing for learning among our students. One such new approach, the VALUE project, using rubrics and portfolios of student work, is described and discussed as a way to engage students in assessing their own leaning, while giving faculty useful information, and institutions reportable results for accountability.

Since We Seem to Agree, Why Are the Outcomes So Difficult to Achieve?

Terry Rhodes

The past five years have witnessed renewed attention to higher education, its importance in preparing individuals to contribute to an educated democracy in a global society, and its necessity for a healthy, competitive, and creative economy. All agree on the need for higher levels of educational completion and attainment. All agree that the students moving through the country's educational pathways are significantly different from those who populated campuses for most of the twentieth century. The evidence is clear that knowledge generation is increasing exponentially, creating a situation where it is no longer possible to encapsulate knowledge within the traditional curriculum. There is wide agreement that the models and practices we in higher education have been using serve many of our students well. But not nearly all of our students benefit. Many observers and their reports point to indicators that our students are falling behind those in other parts of the world in educating for success. At the same time, research in cognitive science, pedagogy, societal change, and personal development is plentiful and useful in pointing to factors that are positively linked to

NEW DIRECTIONS FOR TEACHING AND LEARNING, no. 121, Spring 2010 © Wiley Periodicals, Inc.
Published online in Wiley InterScience (www.interscience.wiley.com) • DOI: 10.1002/tl.384

strategies and practices that promote greater success in learning for the students we are serving.

What, then, prevents higher education from responding more proactively to the demands for change? Many colleagues on many campuses have been engaged in implementing new and important changes in their courses, programs, and even institutions, yet something has been missing to create the systemic change needed to affect national results. Higher education has too often defaulted to calls for simplistic numbers or scores that fit neatly into sound-bites or headlines, but they do not capture the complex and continuous learning that is necessary for success in our technologically driven, global world. What follows is a description of one effort to refocus the national conversation, the intellectual and conceptual frames, and the metrics higher education uses to confront the challenges of providing a liberal education for all of our students.

Agreement on Outcomes

Faculty across the country continue to report that their students need a broad set of essential skills and abilities in addition to a strong knowledge base to achieve success in today's global society. The set of *essential learning outcomes* identified by faculty encompasses not only basic intellectual and practical abilities (such as written, oral, and graphical communication; critical thinking; problem solving; quantitative literacy; and so on) but also individual and personal responsibility outcomes (such as ethical reasoning, intercultural understanding, and working with diverse others, as well as the ability to integrate one's learning across academic boundaries and apply knowledge in unscripted, complex situations).

In a set of surveys conducted by Peter D. Hart Research Associates (AAC&U, 2009), survey responses indicated that employers also look for this same set of essential skills and abilities when hiring the graduates from our colleges and universities. Employers expressed a desire for colleges to do more to develop graduates' preparation in all of the essential learning areas. To demonstrate graduates' achievement of the essential learning outcomes, they expressed a strong desire for evidence that students not only have mastered a body of knowledge but more importantly can apply that knowledge in real-world, nonscripted settings and circumstances.

As a result of this desire for demonstrated learning beyond the traditional classroom, the traditional college transcript is no longer deemed sufficient to reflect level of preparation. Employers are looking for students to have participated in internships and community-based learning opportunities, to have some type of capstone or culminating experience that integrates their learning, and to be able to show actual examples of using their learning to address real problems. Employers indicate that when hiring graduates as new employees they would like to see an example of the prospective employee's senior project, research paper, or internship along with faculty or supervisor evaluation and the student's own reflection on learning. Employers mentioned portfolios of student work as one way for students to present their learning.

Efforts to Report on and Measure Student Learning

In the wake of the Spellings Commission (Miller and Commission, 2006) report on the future of higher education and continuing calls from state and federal policy makers for periodic reporting on the quality of student learning, two higher education associations representing public universities developed a Web-based template for their member institutions to use in reporting information to the public. The Association of Public Land-grant Universities (APLU) and the American Association of State Colleges and Universities (AASCU) developed the Voluntary System of Accountability, or VSA. The actual Web-reporting template, the College Portrait, includes information on cost of attending, retention and graduation rates, and financial aid, tuition, and other cost factors. A second section contains survey information on the student experience at the institution as reflected in, for example, the National Survey of Student Engagement. A final section requires campuses to include information on student learning.

For the student learning section of the College Portrait, institutions must report the results of one of three standard tests: the Measure of Academic Proficiency and Progress (MAPP), the Collegiate Assessment of Academic Proficiency (CAAP), or the Collegiate Learning Assessment (CLA). These three tests are administered to voluntary samples of freshmen and senior students. The tests focus on three primary outcomes: written communication, problem-solving and analysis, and critical thinking. Institutions participating in the VSA may supplement the student learning test results with other types of evidence of student learning used at the specific institution. The National Association of Independent Colleges and Universities (NAICU) developed a similar Web-based template, U-CAN, for use by independent colleges. The U-CAN template does not have a required section for reporting student learning measures.

Each of the standard tests for student learning included in the VSA is administered to a sample of freshmen or seniors at an institution (approximately one to two hundred students in the sample) during a specified time period. These are typically not high-stakes tests; how well a student does on the test has no impact on her or his progress, graduation, or grade point average (GPA). The results are useful as a general indicator at the institutional level, but not at the student level. Students are usually invited to take the test and offered a modest inducement to do so (for example, a book store gift certificate, food, or cash).

In 2007, the Fund for the Improvement of Post Secondary Education (FIPSE) funded a major project, Rising to the Challenge, having three distinct parts: (1) a construct validity study of the VSA, MAPP, CAAP, and

CLA exams for the three outcomes on which they focus (writing, critical thinking, and analysis and problem solving, under the direction of APLU); (2) construction of a new student survey focused on outcomes related to preparation of students for their roles in civic life and employment readiness, the Preparation by Degrees survey (under the direction of AASCU); and (3) development of rubrics for a broad range of fifteen learning outcomes focused on student work gathered through portfolios, or Valid Assessment of Learning in Undergraduate Education (VALUE, under the direction of AAC&U).

The results of the three-pronged project were AASCU's new student survey, focused on learning opportunities and involvement in areas not frequently measured by institutions, such as civic engagement, ethical reasoning, teamwork, and other work and career readiness abilities. The second component, APLU's construct validity study, found that (1) the three tests institutions are required to use as part of the VSA do measure the same three distinct learning outcomes they share; (2) seniors do better on the tests than freshmen; and (3) the mode of testing did not make a significant difference in student performance. The AAAC&U component was a departure from the existing approaches to capturing student learning and is the focus of the remainder of this discussion.

VALUE: Valid Assessment of Learning in Undergraduate Education

As part of AAC&U's LEAP (Liberal Education and America's Promise) initiative to reinvigorate the liberal learning tradition in American colleges and universities, the VALUE project endeavored to determine whether faculty—regardless of the type of institution, its size, mission, mix of students and programs, or location—had similar expectations for learning in all of the areas of learning typically deemed essential for student success.

The project began by recruiting teams of faculty for each of fifteen learning outcomes from institutions across the country, including some student affairs professionals. The rubric development teams then reviewed a collection of existing rubrics in each learning area, obtained through Web searches and calls for campuses and faculty to submit rubrics developed on individual campuses. The review of existing rubrics was undertaken to determine if a set of broadly shared characteristics or aspects of the learning in each area could be identified from the local rubrics. Rubric development team members were then engaged in drafting rubrics on the basis of their research and analysis. More than one hundred faculty participated in the rubric development teams. Faculty then tested the rubric drafts on more than a hundred campuses using collections of student work on their campus. The results of the campus testing were collected and shared with the development teams, who then revised the rubrics according to the testing feedback. A series of two or three retesting cycles with campus student work ensued. The final product was a set of general or meta-rubrics for fifteen essential learning outcomes.

A national panel was convened near the end of the project. The national panel comprised thirty individuals from on and off campus. Some of the campus panelists were familiar with collecting student work through e-portfolios, while others were not. Some had expertise in assessment; others did not. Represented on the panel were employers, graduate students, school teachers, and nonprofit personnel from all parts of the country. None of the panelists had been involved in the project.

For two days, the panelists engaged in learning about three of the VALUE rubrics and applying them to collections of student work for assessment purposes. The first half of the day was spent on an interrater reliability session, which resulted in a commonly accepted result over .80 among the reviewers. Three sets of student work were reviewed using three rubrics to evaluate student performance and the utility of the rubrics. Panelists reviewed e-portfolios of student work from a broad range of institutions, including Research I campuses, comprehensive campuses, private liberal arts campuses, and community colleges. The panelists offered both their analysis of the understandability and usefulness of the rubrics for evaluating student work and actual assessment of the work itself using the rubrics as a performance standard.

The panelists had minimal difficulty in using two of the rubrics. A third generated substantial discussion of terms and meaning, to the point where it was determined it would need significant targeted revision before being ready for general use. As an assessment tool, the rubrics on which there was consensus resulted in a commonly accepted level of agreement on quality or performance of the student work examined; that is, reviewers could use the rubric and had a very high level of agreement on demonstrated achievement. The rubrics were useful for assessing student work regardless of the type of institution, the prestige of the institution, or the type of assignment included in the e-portfolio for review. The national panel results were shared with the rubric development teams and used for additional revisions of the respective rubrics.

The resultant VALUE rubrics were envisioned as an encapsulation of broadly shared core elements identified as abilities necessary to demonstrate learning in each of the outcome areas. The rubrics were considered useful at the institutional level as written, not at the course or assignment level, nor for grading student work. The rubrics were developed with the intent to use them with a collection of student work over time to examine and demonstrate students' learning throughout their educational pathways. The most advanced level of demonstrated learning was expectation for accomplishment as students approached attainment of a baccalaureate degree, while the first level was viewed as representing expectations reflective of current student accomplishment in their first year of undergraduate performance. The rubrics represent a developmental assumption for learning in postsecondary education, and the reality that learning is multifaceted and nuanced and not linear—advancing and receding as students mature, change foci of study, and practice various skills and abilities while moving through the curriculum and co-curriculum and among or between institutions. The rubrics are artificial in that learning does not occur in the discrete packages encompassed by individual rubrics. However, by articulating learning in each area, the overlap and the importance of key dimensions of learning are revealed as integrative or distinctive as they take form as a set of important learning skills and abilities.

The VALUE project demonstrated that nationally there are broadly shared expectations for learning among faculty regardless of where they teach; that there are multiple key elements or facets to learning in every outcome area; and that student work needs to be the focus of any assessment of student learning because it represents what our institutions actually engage with as important work and it is where students will try to demonstrate their best learning. The VALUE rubrics were found to be useful with a broad range of assignments, fields of study, years of attendance, modes of representing student work, and type of institution. The rubrics are a beginning for campus and national conversations around student learning that present a way for faculty on a campus or in a program to translate the general rubrics into the concepts and language of the program or discipline, and to add specific factors for learning reflective of the particulars of a course or individual assignment. Further, the rubrics furnish a mechanism for individual faculty and programs to place their judgments within a nationally shared context that both confirms and reflects the expert judgment of faculty.

Importantly, articulation of expected learning through a rubric allows students to have a better idea of what the skills and abilities associated with collegiate learning look like across the key dimensions of learning in the essential outcome areas that faculty and employers seek in graduates. The power of having a shared language for learning permits faculty from a number of departments and programs to talk with one another about student learning and their own pedagogies and assignments, while at the same time helping students join in a common dialogue and exploration of what quality learning looks like in practice.

Making Learning Excellence Inclusive

Through the research emerging from ten years of administering the NSSE (National Survey of Student Engagement) on high-impact practices (Kuh, 2008), there is evidence that when students have the opportunity to participate in a set of engaging pedagogies—for example, learning communities, undergraduate research, community-based learning, capstone projects, and so on—learning is deepened and improved. In particular, our students who are least well prepared on entrance appear to experience reported learning gains greater than the better prepared students who engaged at the same level. Yet at present we tend to reserve opportunities for students to participate in the array of high-impact practices for the most talented students on our campuses.

Additionally, the Wabash National Study of Liberal Arts Education findings suggest a similar trend in learning. The early findings from their project identified three best practices scales that correlated positively with student learning: good teaching, academic challenge, and diversity experiences. In their research, they found that these broad categories of teaching practice and institutional culture "predict growth on a wide variety of student outcomes including leadership, openness to diversity and challenge, political and social involvement, and positive attitude toward literacy" (National Study of Liberal Arts Education, 2009). They also found that students in their first year overwhelmingly indicated having only moderate or limited exposure to these important pedagogies and interactions, although students who reported having the most exposure and involvement in the practices also reported the highest gains in learning, further suggesting the desirability of offering engaging learning experiences early and often for our students.

Integrating Student Learning

Many campuses are exploring use of student e-portfolios to engage students in their learning throughout the curriculum and co-curriculum, and even across institutional boundaries as students enter and leave colleges and attend multiple institutions at the same time. By creating frameworks—the e-portfolio—through which students can gather all or a portion of the work they produce, and in which faculty, if desired, can record their assessment of the work, and in which students can reflect on the quality of their work in relation to the expected learning, it is possible to view the topography and progress of student learning throughout and across the student's educational experience. By asking students to reflect on their learning and point to where and how they are demonstrating their learning in all or some of the essential learning outcomes, students are encouraged to view their learning in a larger context than a single assignment or course, to view their work as part of a larger design shared across the curriculum, and hopefully the institution. E-portfolios allow faculty also to have the advantage of both seeing how their teaching is affecting student learning in relation to what the student brings to the particular course or piece of the picture, and how the various outcomes for essential learning are linked and joined across the student experience.

Use of e-portfolios of student work also recognizes the multiple ways in which students learn and express their learning in a contemporary world. Multiple modes and media for teaching and learning need to be included if we are to truly capture the divergent ways in which the students we have at our institutions engage in finding, understanding, and communicating their learning. The high-impact practices that are linked to enhanced learning for students as reflected in the NSSE and Wabash National Study findings also lend themselves well to the representational capabilities of e-portfolios, especially the capability of having students point to and reflect on where, how, and why their learning was affected through participation in the practices.

Liberal Learning on Campus Today

Traditionally, the part of an undergraduate education that all students partake of is general education, or what we refer to as liberal learning. It encompasses learning in important knowledge areas *and* practical and intellectual skills and abilities (writing, speaking, quantitative literacy, critical thinking, analysis and problem solving), teamwork, personal and social responsibility (ethical decision making, civic engagement, intercultural understanding and competence, lifelong learning), and the ability to integrate one's learning across general and specialized studies. Faculty members across the country support the many aspects of liberal learning. Employers, in their own language, support a similar listing of essential learning for graduates. Studies from the Georgetown Center on Education and the Workforce on the relationship between liberal learning and economic contribution (Carnevale, 2009) and impact also support the positive impact of liberal learning. A consensus on the need for liberal learning as an organizing focus for our campuses exists.

The part of the curriculum we call general education has become the foundational starting place for campuses seeking to focus their efforts to restructure and reconceptualize their approaches to learning. Campuses are beginning to recognize that the inoculation approach to learning—writing is important, so take a composition course; quantitative literacy is critical, so take a math course—is quite limited in its impact. Simply checking the boxes no longer suffices as learning. Deep learning that is retained and usable develops over time and through practice in multiple settings under differing circumstances. Hence, campuses are scaffolding learning throughout the curriculum, and across the years at progressively more sophisticated levels of accomplishment, in both general education and the major.

Use of rubrics constructed on the basis of complex dimensions of learning over time that are demonstrated through the work we ask our students to do as part of their curriculum and co-curriculum begins to offer a framework and a means for accomplishing the learning we desire. Institutional outcomes and rubrics that articulate the associated learning can be used to frame the detailed description of learning expectations at the program, course, and assignment levels, thus allowing faculty to grade student progress and performance while at the same time supplying the aggregation of scores and performance information for programmatic and institutional reporting required by various internal and external audiences. When student work is collected through an e-portfolio, examples of what the rubrics and performance levels actually look like in practice can be associated directly with formative as well as summative representations of student learning. This approach begins to transform assessment from a compliance burden to an integral part of student and faculty work that is a powerful practice for improving teaching and learning.

The evidence is overwhelming that we have broadly shared understanding of what good learning looks like, we have the evidence that supports powerful pedagogies, and we have the capacity to collect, assess, and communicate the kinds of learning our students can do. Indeed, faculty across the country are already engaging in the teaching and learning we say we want and need. Improved teaching and learning is happening. We need look no further than the chapters in this volume. We simply need to embrace our role as professionals engaged in educating a diverse and talented student body that is distinctly different from the students of the last century and that needs to be prepared for the challenges of a society. As former Secretary of Education Richard Riley memorably put it, "we are currently preparing students for jobs that don't yet exist . . . using technologies that haven't been invented . . . in order to solve problems that we don't even know are problems yet (cited in Tritelli, 2009)." No single score or number can represent the kinds of liberal learning necessary to meet this reality.

References

AAC&U. (2009). Trends and emerging practices in general education. Retrieved October 1, 2008, from http://www.aacu.org/membership/documents/2009Member Survey_Part2.pdf.

Carnevale, T. (2009). *College is still the best option.* Center on Education in the Workforce. Retrieved September 22, 2009, from http://cew.georgetown.edu/resources/ presentations/.

Kuh, G. (2008). *High impact practices and student learning.* Washington, DC: Association of American Colleges and Universities.

Miller, C., and Commission (2006). A Test of Leadership: Charting the Future of U.S. Higher Education. Retrieved January 4, 2010, from http://www.ed.gov/about/ bdscomm/list/hiedfuture/reports/final-report.pdf.

National Study of Liberal Arts Education. (2009). *High impact practices and experiences from the Wabash National Study.* Retrieved September 22, 2009, from http://www .liberalarts.wabash.edu/study-research/.

Tritelli, D. (2009). From the editor, *Liberal Education, 95*(1), 4.

TERRY RHODES *received his B.A. from Indiana University at Bloomington and his M.A. and Ph.D. in Political Science from the University of North Carolina at Chapel Hill. Before moving into national higher education work, he was a faculty member for twenty-five years. Dr. Rhodes is currently vice president for the Office of Quality, Curriculum and Assessment at the Association of American Colleges and Universities (AAC&U) where he focuses on the quality of undergraduate education, access, general education, and assessment of student learning. He is also director of the annual AAC&U General Education Institute.*

3

When the University of North Dakota began working to improve general education, two concerns were recognized. The first issue, which faculty and administrators across campus found immediately engaging, was how to change general education so that it would be a better program, more likely to yield clear student learning benefits. A second concern, less obvious but ultimately more significant, was how to make general education really matter. This cross-campus faculty engagement in general education goals has been extremely energizing, essentially making the program matter to faculty across disciplines; and this heightened faculty interest is already translating to students as faculty engage more purposefully with the program.

Making General Education Matter: Structures and Strategies

Joan Hawthorne, Anne Kelsch, Tom Steen

A few years ago, in the midst of a multiyear study of general education, a professor involved in the research articulated a finding that had become inescapable: it seemed few students believed general education was relevant. Students did not perceive that their University of North Dakota (UND) faculty valued general education, and they themselves, outside of vaguely supportive but probably gratuitous remarks about the "importance of a well-rounded education," couldn't identify much that was productive about their experience with the program. In the view of students participating in the study, general education simply wasn't significant. What could be done to make a general education program matter to those engaged with it?

We kept that question at the forefront of our minds during our subsequent general education reform, and one outcome of our focus was development of a program that integrated general education goals into many majors, offering extensive opportunities for faculty and students to invest in the goals beyond the first- and second-year curriculum. Although it now appears vital, the need for longitudinal integration became apparent only in hindsight.

The symptoms of inadequate integration should have been obvious. Students' dismissive comments about general education were one signal.

NEW DIRECTIONS FOR TEACHING AND LEARNING, no. 121, Spring 2010   © Wiley Periodicals, Inc.
Published online in Wiley InterScience (www.interscience.wiley.com) • DOI: 10.1002/tl.385

23

General education was disconnected from degree programs and professional majors. Faculty typically viewed courses included in the general education program as an introduction to the major; "counting" as general education was a distinctly secondary focus, and helping students achieve general education learning goals often failed to register at all. Yet it was only in contrast to the new program that we recognized the degree to which these symptoms indicated a systematic problem: lack of integration between general education and the broader undergraduate curriculum.

In this chapter, we tell the story of how this realization emerged and describe the changes that not only made general education matter more but perhaps most important succeeded in integrating the program across the institution.

The Student Perspective: Data Collection, Part One

University of North Dakota faculty gleaned many insights regarding student attitudes about general education through a six-year study of student perceptions of the general education program and their learning around its cross-disciplinary goals. The associate provost initiated the General Education Longitudinal Study (GELS), funded by a Bush Foundation grant, in 2000. The study followed a decision to conduct an initial assessment of student learning in our GE program using locally developed qualitative measures, rather than quantitative or standardized instruments. This choice reflected the perceived inadequacy of available instruments to effectively document the complex nature of learning around all of our cross-disciplinary goals. However, decision makers also recognized that such learning might occur through activities and experiences outside of general education courses—by way of co-curricular activities, for example, or within courses taken for the major. A longitudinal study based on student experiences would permit fuller understanding of how they achieved intended general education outcomes, whether within the general education curriculum or beyond.

A team of ten faculty members conducted the study, interviewing each student participant (approximately 120 interviewees) once every semester. Interviews were semistructured, allowing flexibility within the context of the focus on student perceptions of their learning related to general education goals. Interviewers stayed open to any insights students might offer regarding people, places, and activities related to their learning.

In addition to conducting interviews, the team wrote the interview scripts, conducted a yearly analysis, and made annual campus presentations of findings. As well, they contributed to a final report that argued for institutional change, noting that

it is important to reaffirm these common [interdisciplinary] goals and bring new life and meaning to the ways we address them within the University. One way to do this is to make the concept of general education, its purposes and meanings, both more visible and more fully embedded in the culture of UND [Hanhan et al., 2004].

The team's further recommendations were sharp and dispiriting. For example, they reported that students rarely identified courses taken for general education credit as the site of their learning around the cross-disciplinary general education goals and often described such courses as an incidental, or even irritating, distraction en route to their degree. Although seniors did report substantial progress toward achieving general education outcomes, they most often traced that learning to venues external to the general education program: the major, extracurricular activities, and personal experiences such as employment. Despite the program's rhetoric and intent, students typically perceived general education courses as, at best, conveying fundamental content knowledge. More often, they saw them as something to get out of the way so they could get on with the "real" academic work of their chosen program.

Not only did some significant percentage of UND's students perceive the general education program as unimportant, they also did not value specific individual goals. The goal they cared least about was "achieving a familiarity with cultures other than their own." Ironically, although faculty valued this goal highly, students believed that their teachers shared their disregard. So although faculty claimed to support the goals, they had done little to convince students of their worth. Not surprisingly, those conducting the study and reviewing its findings believed it established a strong need for program reform.

Expanding Our Understanding: Data Collection, Part Two

With that rather bleak perspective as a backdrop, others collected additional kinds of data about achievement of general education goals. The General Education Requirements Committee (GERC), which oversees course validations, conducted a survey of departments offering general education courses. The survey revealed which goals were intended to be addressed in courses that "counted" in the program. The registrar's office furnished a random sample of transcripts from recent graduates, and analysis of those transcripts, matched up against findings from the goals survey, showed how many courses aiming at a given goal were taken by each student in the sample. Faculty teams gathered to plan assessmen projects that would directly evaluate the work of seniors on three general education goals: critical thinking, written communication, and cultural awareness. Results presented a snapshot of graduating students' performance on those key goals, including specific areas of strength and weakness within each goal.

Simply planning these projects was useful. To conduct direct assessments, faculty wrestled with the fact that UND did not define the general education goals with any specificity. What did we mean, really, by "problem solving," and how was that different from "critical thinking"? What criteria could be used to define "cultural familiarity," and how did that relate to our "world cultures" requirement (apparently added in support of the cultural familiarity goal)? We didn't know. We recognized too that faculty teaching general education classes were similarly uncertain. Surely, we concluded, part of the reason students were so vague about and disengaged from the general education program was that faculty were far from clear about either its meaning or its purpose.

As data came in from the assessments, results corroborated and extended what we had learned from students. Students really did experience considerably less emphasis on cultural familiarity than on any other goal, for example. Depending on course choices, students could easily have quite different experiences with the general education goals. Few students demonstrated learning at the very bottom level defined by the rubrics, but some really did score that low. Others were very low on specific criteria. According to all of these measures, our program was ripe for reform.

Initiating General Education Reform. General education reform processes include common elements (see, Gano-Phillips & Barnett, 2009; Kanter, Gamson, & London, 1997), and many of those elements characterized our reform effort as well. We started by appointing a task force that included wide campus representation. Members met more frequently (usually every other week) and over a longer period of time (two years) than was originally anticipated. Their first step was a review of findings from general education assessments. Task force members also solicited input from individuals and programs, even making phone calls to various campus departments and essentially inviting themselves to departmental meetings for extended conversation about general education. Members attended national meetings, trolled Web sites, read articles and books about general education and reform, and engaged in lengthy conversation with campus stakeholders.

Identifying Program Goals. Eventually task force members debated goals, an extensive process that required about nine months of discussion prior to consensus. Some of the goals agreed to, we believed, would automatically be addressed in any revised curriculum without requiring special efforts. Many UND courses, for example, might be expected to address critical thinking. Other goals were more worrisome.

We already knew from the longitudinal study and transcript analysis that our old cultural familiarity goal had been haphazardly and infrequently addressed. We knew from members of the GERC (the program oversight committee) that faculty validating courses for GE and faculty serving on the GERC did not always agree on the meaning of cultural familiarity. For example, some courses that faculty identified as addressing cultural familiarity appeared, to committee members, instead to reinforce stereotypes (e.g., a course using popular movies to illustrate "common traits" of a particular ethnic group). Lacking a definition for the goal, it was impossible to achieve resolution in a completely satisfactory and fair way. How could we avoid creating similar issues within a new program? Goals needed to be more explicit, with wording that made sense to students and faculty alike, and each goal needed a defining rubric that could be used to assess learning related to it. But how could learning around diversity, however named and defined, be strengthened within the new program?

Our communication goal was a similarly instructive example. Although the only courses specified in our old program were Composition I and Composition II, faculty across campus had uniformly reported that our students needed stronger writing skills. Additional composition classes were not a plausible option, given credit-hour constraints within professional programs. Nor, even if required, was it likely that more of the same would fix the problem. How might we do better?

Discussion about new goals raised similar questions. As a plan for the new program took form, we agreed to add a quantitative reasoning (QR) goal. But its adoption led to another consideration: How could we design the new program to ensure that all students were given opportunities to achieve the intended learning? Even those students who are "good at" math often avoid courses requiring its application to real-world problems. Yet we agreed that a QR goal should be about the appropriate application of mathematical concepts rather than computation itself, so where would students gain that experience?

Developing Special Emphasis Requirements. Faced with questions such as these, task force members agreed that, to help students achieve the kinds of learning targeted by some program goals, courses with an explicit focus on specified outcomes would be necessary. We arrived at a structural solution: general education would consist of two overlapping layers, one addressing breadth requirements and a second, in support of specific program goals, addressing what we began to call special emphasis requirements.

The breadth requirements would align with the North Dakota system's mandated distribution of GE credits. Early in the reform process task force members had considered challenging the state mandate, but they decided to work within its constraints. This decision was partly pragmatic, but most members also valued a breadth-of-study requirement. The state system specified a typical division of general education courses into four disciplinary categories. As long as credit requirements within those categories were met, the system gave institutions freedom to allow students to choose from a menu or impose additional restrictions and requirements. Although UND's old general education program, closely based on the state model, had theoretically allowed tremendous freedom in course selection, specific majors imposed significant constraints on students' choices. For example, nursing identified three specific courses students must take to meet the required nine credit hours in the social sciences.

Furthermore, one danger of a breadth-based system was that the system structure implied that the disciplines were primary. The general education program cross-disciplinary goals felt like an afterthought or add-on. In fact, we knew from our data analysis that the old program had functioned that way. In many general education courses, program goals were addressed only marginally, with minimal assurance that students achieved exposure to (let alone competency on) general education goals.

The second layer in the new general education program was designed to address that problem. This layer, made up of special emphasis requirements, would further an explicit focus on cross-disciplinary goals that might otherwise be underemphasized, depending on the student's major and choices. In the old program, students had to take a course (unfortunately ill-defined) intended to promote exposure to "world cultures." They were also required to take two composition courses in support of the written communication goal. In the new program, task force members agreed, we would build on and improve that general idea with additional goal-specific requirements.

In support of the revised social-cultural diversity goal, students would be required to take a course focused on U.S. diversity (designated with a U) and another focused on global diversity (G). These courses might fall within or outside of the distribution (breadth) component of general education. Students would take an oral communication (O) course—not necessarily a speech course, and not necessarily taught within the communication program—to develop skills in that area. An advanced communication course (A) would be taken after Comp I, Comp II, and the O course to emphasize skills at a higher level than those more basic classes. A required course focusing on quantitative reasoning (QR) would not necessarily be taught within math, and in fact not all math courses would likely "count" for the QR requirement.

These special emphasis requirements would differ from the old requirements in that there would be definitions for them and standards to describe expectations for courses that could count toward meeting the requirements. For example, a specified percentage of the course content, activities, assignments, and grading would need to be organized around the GE goal. Assessment data regarding students' achievement of the specified outcome would be required during course revalidation. Rather than leave each individual instructor to determine the goal's meaning, a clear definition would be supplied and, when requesting validation for the requirement, the instructor would need to demonstrate how his or her course aligned with that definition and other specifications.

The special emphasis requirements, task force members believed, would ensure that the cross-disciplinary goals were concrete. They would require both students and faculty to take the goals seriously. They would emphasize outcomes that were generally agreed to be critical but that could nevertheless fall through the cracks of a student's university education.

Developing a GE Capstone. An additional component of the special emphasis layer would be a senior-level general education capstone ensuring that the general education program was integrated across the undergraduate curriculum. This requirement also introduced a means of reinforcing our program for students who transferred in with most of their GE credits in place. We anticipated that most departments, preferring to retain control of senior curricula, would choose to offer the general education capstone within the major, thereby integrating GE into specific programs as well as across the undergraduate experience.

The capstone paved the way for a considerably more integrated general education program. But in ways we did not fully anticipate, other aspects of the special emphasis requirements have more quietly had a similar effect on our undergraduate curricula.

Implementing the New Requirements. From the outset the task force conceived of the capstone as a concrete means of integration. However, they gave less thought initially to how the special emphasis requirements would fit within a student's overall plan of study. The new general education program, practically speaking, could not exceed the thirty-nine credits required by the old program because the curricula of some majors (engineering, nursing) were already so constrained by professional accreditation requirements—combined with state board expectations that undergraduate degree programs be manageable within four years—that no additional credits could be added. Moreover, the extremely tight curricula meant that students in such majors had very few "free" credits for taking courses of personal interest, and task force members were reluctant to further limit their choice.

Conversations about credit constraints, in fact, had been an important factor prompting our consideration of "overlays": special emphasis courses that could be taken within the mandated breadth requirements. We believed that plans of study developed by various departments would be adapted to guide students in efficiently combining breadth and special emphasis requirements, along with prerequisites for the major. Courses meeting the QR requirement, for example, could overlay courses taken to meet social sciences requirements.

We also anticipated that departments might choose to offer some of these special emphasis courses for their own majors. Although we had assured faculty that individual departments would not be required to offer a general education capstone (meaning that some nonmajor-specific general education capstone courses would be necessary), we believed that most departments would opt to develop their own capstone focusing on goals for learning both within the major and within general education. Several departments, we predicted, would take advantage of the opportunity to develop a course within the major that emphasized communication in the discipline, meeting the new advanced communication requirement within the capstone.

What we did not foresee was the degree of enthusiasm departments would bring to the idea of meeting additional special emphasis requirements within their curricula, thus infusing general education goals more strongly into majors. For example, in occupational therapy and social work faculty were already teaching courses that emphasized social-cultural diversity; they were interested in reconceiving those courses to offer major-specific opportunities for students to meet new general education diversity requirements. Other departments required research methods courses, which faculty realized could, with minimal redevelopment, meet the quantitative reasoning requirement. Faculty in engineering departments proposed to strengthen the emphasis on oral communication in order to meet the O requirement in their senior-level courses.

Reflecting on What's Been Learned. Plans are one thing; translating them into action is another. As we implement our new program, we take special notice of how departments and their faculty members are adapting to what we are now calling the "essential studies" program. One immediate effect of the new requirements is that many departments are moving quickly to create their own general education capstones. Besides using courses that already function as a departmental or disciplinary capstone as their general education capstone (a strategy that requires only modest adjustments), a number of programs are developing new capstones, sometimes creating courses that bridge all the various tracks or subdisciplines in their majors. These capstones will foster integration of at least two kinds: in some cases, they will integrate students who, because of differing career paths within a department, have rarely been in classes together (for example, our aviation major has tracks for pilots, air traffic controllers, airport managers, and meteorologists, all of whom will be brought together in their new general education capstone). In other situations, faculty are reenvisioning current courses into capstones that will consciously emphasize general education program goals. Social work majors, for example, will find that a new reflective component enhances an existing experiential component, thus fulfilling both major and general education capstone requirements.

A second effect of implementing the new program has been the effort, across many more departments than originally envisioned, to integrate special emphasis requirements into the major. Courses meeting these requirements can be met within traditional general education-providing departments such as English, music, psychology, and mathematics, but they can also be met through courses offered in physical therapy, civil engineering, and clinical lab science. Students in those programs can expect to be reminded of general education goals as they work through the major. They will find opportunities to practice skills encountered in classes taken as part of the GE breadth requirements as they move forward into classes in their program. General education will become a longitudinal part of the undergraduate curriculum rather than a preliminary experience that paves the way for "real work" within the major.

These changes, of course, also create challenges. One such challenge is the need to help faculty understand the new program. Faculty long accustomed to viewing general education as distinct from the major need to be reminded that they may want to consider revising a course to meet special emphasis requirements. In the English department, for example, despite a course list that includes several in both advanced composition and creative writing, it was not intuitively obvious to faculty that their courses could, and indeed should, be validated for the new advanced communication requirement. Faculty thought of those courses as part of the major, and we've learned that we need to increase our efforts in faculty development to promote new possibilities for integrating the work within disciplines with that of general education.

Another challenge rests with our Essential Studies Committee, the body charged with the responsibility for approving ("validating") and reapproving ("revalidating") courses that can be used to meet GE requirements. When committee members see a course with a title like Fluid Mechanics proposed for general education validation (perhaps to meet an O or Q requirement), the first reaction has sometimes been "That's not general education." We on the committee are learning to ask ourselves, "But could it be?" If we consider such a course as a replacement for the traditional breadth requirement, it feels inappropriate. If we consider instead that students may more readily and enthusiastically learn to apply quantitative concepts or communicate effectively when the topic is one they take seriously or think about in terms of their chosen profession, then our answer might be different. But still the bottom line needs to be, "What do they learn? How much is that emphasized? Is it 'required' of students [built into the testing] or taught and practiced?" Working through these questions has been helpful, and over this first year we've developed definitions and standards to help us stay focused on these key issues.

In spite of challenges, implementation of the new program has already resulted in some pleasant surprises, many of which have occurred in our professional departments. Although these departments are often left out of general education programs, at least in terms of contributing to course offerings, we've found that faculty in professional fields are very supportive of general education goals. Given a reason to more explicitly focus on those goals, and the opportunity to be part of the program, many such faculty are modifying courses to more explicitly emphasize general education goals.

Another unexpected benefit of integrating general education into the major is the impact on transfer students. It's important for all graduates of a college or university to be given the opportunity to achieve learning specified in that institution's general education goals. Yet many transfer students will have completed the first year or two, or even more, of the undergraduate curriculum elsewhere (perhaps at multiple institutions) and transfer in those credits. However worthy the individual courses, they were never intended to add up in any specific way, and they certainly were not chosen to help the student achieve specific learning outcomes specified by UND.

Although we conceived the capstone as one means of ensuring that our graduates, both transfer and "home-grown," would receive explicit focus on our general education goals, we don't require that capstones address all general education goals (addressing all, we feared, would inevitably result in a superficial "exposure" level of emphasis). However, if a social work student has taken a research course that was redesigned to include a focus on quantitative reasoning, a client-relationship course focused on U.S. diversity, and a capstone course emphasizing communication and critical thinking, we can feel confident in that student's learning around our general education goals. A chemical engineering student who transfers in the first two years of her curriculum and then takes ChE courses developed to emphasize oral and advanced communication, with a capstone focused on critical thinking and information literacy, will have had a reasonable opportunity to benefit from our general education program. Such a student will graduate with a more coherent emphasis on UND's general education goals, integrated within disciplinary requirements and outcomes.

Does General Education Matter More Now? Our two-layer approach has ultimately served to make general education matter more at UND. Although our revised program is young, we believe that students are encountering general education in a new way with requirements that align not just with disciplines but also with goals and learning outcomes. The demarcation between general education and majors is no longer sharp. As opposed to students getting general education courses out of the way in their first years, they are taking courses with a strong emphasis on general education outcomes at the upper-division level, often in the context of the subject matter most interesting to them. Their general education experience is more vertical and intentional, connections across the curriculum are more obvious, and GE goals often feel more relevant and practical thanks to clear connections faculty are making between those goals and disciplin--ary content.

Faculty are paying more attention to general education, too. The standards required to achieve validation of courses are higher, with direct assessment of clearly articulated goals required as part of revalidation. Because more departments are offering courses to meet the special emphasis requirements, general education goals are being integrated at all levels of the curriculum and in courses taught by a greater range of faculty. The general education capstone commonly doubles as a disciplinary capstone, so departments are focused in a new way on general education outcomes. We hope that more departments will deliberately incorporate general education goals into program goals, thus further enhancing a sense of integration and relevancy. The goals are also serving as organizing units that bring together faculty and staff with shared interests (as with emphasizing information literacy) for discussion of teaching and learning related to that goal.

NEW DIRECTIONS FOR TEACHING AND LEARNING • DOI: 10.1002/tl

So for now, we can say that on our campus general education matters more to both faculty and students. The long-range challenge, of course, will be to sustain the energy and effort that has come along with the spirit of innovation and newness, and to continue to find ways to develop and improve our essential studies program.

References

Gano-Phillips, S., & Barnett, R. (Eds.). (2009). *A process approach to general education reform: Transforming institutional culture*. Madison, WI: Atwood Publishing.
Hanhan, S., Kelsch, A., Anderegg, J., Ballantine, T., Byram, D., Fink, K., et al. (2004). *University of North Dakota Bush Longitudinal Study: What students tell us about cross-disciplinary general education goals and learning*. University of North Dakota. Retrieved from http://www.und.edu/dept/oid/getf_assessment.htm on October 8, 2009.
Kanter, S. L., Gamson, Z. F., & London, H. B. (1997). *Revitalizing general education in a time of scarcity: A navigational chart for administrators and faculty*. Boston: Allyn and Bacon.

JOAN HAWTHORNE *is the assistant provost at the University of North Dakota, where she has oversight for assessment of student learning among other responsibilities. Dr. Hawthorne previously served as coordinator for Writing Across the Curriculum and the Writing Center. Her teaching responsibilities have been in Teaching and Learning (where she developed a graduate course on Assessment in Higher Education), Educational Foundations and Research, and English. Her Ph.D. is in Curriculum and Instruction—Higher Education.*

ANNE KELSCH *is the director of Instructional Development at the University of North Dakota. She is an associate professor of History and has been teaching at UND since 1994. She earned her Ph.D. in European History from Texas A&M University in 1993, and her historical research focuses on social and gender identity in 19th and 20th century Britain. Her research interests are in pedagogy, and she has presented at national and international conferences on student learning.*

TOM STEEN *is an associate professor and coordinator of P.E. Teacher Education at the University of North Dakota. He is responsible for the teacher education program in physical education. Besides teaching the department's "methods" courses, he also teaches graduate courses, with special emphasis on instructional strategies, curriculum development, and sport education. He received his Ph.D. from The Ohio State University.*

NEW DIRECTIONS FOR TEACHING AND LEARNING • DOI: 10.1002/tl

4

At North Carolina State University, inquiry-guided learning offered a compelling framework for integrating the undergraduate curriculum across general education and the major. Rather than adopting a definition of inquiry-guided learning as a prescribed set of approaches, participating faculty and staff members agreed on four overarching intended learning outcomes as the distinctive feature of inquiry-guided learning: critical thinking, habits of independent inquiry, taking responsibility for one's own learning, and intellectual growth and maturity. Regardless of discipline, faculty members were able to translate the outcomes readily into terms that had meaning within their disciplinary context. As a result the outcomes offered a common language that provided unity to the undergraduate experience for faculty members and ultimately for students.

Unifying the Undergraduate Curriculum Through Inquiry-Guided Learning

Virginia S. Lee, Sarah Ash

The inquiry-guided learning (IGL) initiative at North Carolina State University was a multifaceted faculty development effort that engaged more than two hundred faculty and more than sixty academic and administrative units on campus. In addition, this program affected more than six thousand students. The initiative focused on a growing First Year Inquiry Program that reached approximately one-third of incoming freshmen; a First Year Seminar Program in the College of Humanities and Social Sciences; selected courses throughout the undergraduate program, both in general education and the major; and nine lead departments in seven of the university's ten colleges that introduced inquiry-guided learning into a sequence of courses in the major.

Participating faculty members designed courses that facilitated learning through students' active investigation of complex questions and problems and, in the process, promoted four broad student learning outcomes: critical thinking, developing habits of independent inquiry, responsibility

NEW DIRECTIONS FOR TEACHING AND LEARNING, no. 121, Spring 2010 © Wiley Periodicals, Inc.
Published online in Wiley InterScience (www.interscience.wiley.com) • DOI: 10.1002/tl.386

for one's own learning, and intellectual growth and development. A shared commitment to these outcomes furthered integration of the IGL initiative with three other key efforts on campus: writing and speaking across the curriculum, undergraduate academic program review, and assessment. The initiative was also intertwined with broader conversations concerning general education and the undergraduate education curriculum (Lee, 2004b).

In a large research university, a focus on four broad student learning outcomes coupled with a flexible, shared understanding of inquiry-guided learning (Hewlett Steering Committee, 2004) permitted integration of inquiry-guided learning into general education courses as well as courses in the major, which in turn opened the way for greater integration of the undergraduate curriculum. We believe integration across general education and the major never would have been possible had we attempted to agree on a single model of inquiry-guided learning or a prescribed set of approaches.

Originally conceived as an effort to offer students explicit guidance in critical thinking and to hold them accountable for their learning in general education courses, the IGL initiative gained traction in the academic major as well. Regardless of their academic department, instructors were able to translate these outcomes into terms that made sense in their disciplines.

Below are sets of outcomes developed by academic programs related to critical thinking and habits of independent inquiry that describe what students majoring in three disciplines should be able to do when they graduate:

Food Science
- Identify, define, and analyze a problem: what generates the problem, what is given, what is unknown, and what the criteria are for viable solutions to the problem.
- Determine what information is appropriate to solving the problem and then find it, assess its authority and validity, and use it effectively.
- Integrate and apply basic science and mathematics as well as food sciences to the solution of problems in food systems.
- Offer a range of potential viable solutions to the problem.
- Evaluate the solutions according to established criteria, choose the most viable solution, and make a convincing case for that solution.

History
- Pose an interesting research question about history.
- Locate relevant primary and secondary sources for investigating a research question.
- Critically evaluate primary and secondary sources in terms of credibility, authenticity, interpretive stance, audience, potential biases, and value for answering the research question.
- Marshall evidence from the research to support a historical argument for an answer to a research question.

Art and Design
- Understanding of basic design principles, concepts, media, and formats in various fine arts disciplines.
- Mastery of basic foundation techniques, particularly as related to specific fine arts fields.
- Conceive, design, and create works in one or more specific fine arts fields.
- Demonstrate a working knowledge of various production methods and their relationship to conceptualization, development, and completion of works of art.
- Understand the similarities, differences, and relationships among the various fine arts areas.

A meta-analysis of curricular-level outcomes developed by faculty members in each academic program also demonstrated the pervasiveness of the ability to think critically and inquire in ways appropriate to the discipline throughout the undergraduate curriculum. Identification of certain themes (identifying and analyzing a problem, asking pertinent questions, identifying hypotheses, designing experiments) presented four categories of inquiry—problem solving, empirical inquiry, research from sources, and performance—that pervade the undergraduate curriculum (Blanchard, Bresciani, Carter, Lee, & Luginbuhl, 2004).

Faculty Participation

In a research university with an incentive structure overwhelmingly skewed toward research, strategies for getting and sustaining faculty participation in a teaching reform initiative were varied. Generally speaking, participation emerged from a combination of impulses from the grassroots and support and incentives from administration, creating a climate that encouraged innovation in teaching. In addition, an initial grant from the William and Flora Hewlett Foundation followed by funding from the Office of the Provost for a second-generation project gave early support for introduction of inquiry-guided learning into general education courses. A second Hewlett grant supported integration of inquiry-guided learning into courses in selected academic majors.

The earliest stage of the initiative illustrates the interaction of individual initiative, support of administration, and the role of grants very well. In 1996, a graduate student in the Division of Undergraduate Affairs, who also lent support to the Council on Undergraduate Education (CUE), recognized that the university required students to think critically, but that very few faculty members gave students explicit guidance on how to do so. She persuaded a dozen faculty members to attend a two-day workshop on critical thinking given by Richard Paul, with financial support from the dean. The workshop was constructively irritating, and the participating faculty members, who had bonded over the weekend (including sharing a van ride and a legendary dinner at a Thai restaurant), agreed to keep meeting and sharing ideas. Soon after, CUE adopted a position statement on increasing student responsibility for their own learning that described explicitly the role of instructors and students in the learning process (NC State University Council on Undergraduate Education, 2004).

In December 1996, the provost received an invitation to apply for a grant from the Hewlett Foundation to improve general education at a Research I institution and passed it on to the chair of CUE. The chair worked with a small committee and a grant writer on a proposal that brought the emphasis on critical thinking and student responsibility for their own learning under the banner of inquiry-guided learning. They made the case that these emphases could appear on a continuum of inquiry from early general education courses to capstone experiences in the major (Greene, Lee, & Wellman, 2004).

As the initiative unfolded, other factors encouraged faculty participation and persistence, creating a general climate that encouraged innovation:

- A perceived discrepancy between student learning outcomes (e.g., critical thinking, developing habits of independent inquiry) and traditional teaching practices such as lecturing (see Lee, Hyman, & Luginbuhl, 2007)
- Financial incentives in the form of payment for retreats and conference travel and minigrants to departments
- A competitive application process for instructors and departments to participate in grant-funded projects
- Recognition that inquiry-guided learning prompted a desired level and quality of student engagement not possible with traditional teaching methods
- A desire for a sense of community among faculty members interested in teaching
- The success and reputation of previous initiatives that created a desire among other faculty members to participate
- The convergence of mandated reforms such as the introduction of writing and speaking outcomes in the major, undergraduate program review, and requirements of selected disciplinary accrediting bodies such as ABET that were consistent with IGL outcomes and practices
- Support of the administration, e.g., funding of release time for faculty members teaching smaller, First Year Inquiry courses, and a shift in incentive structure in isolated departments and colleges
- A general climate that supported innovation in teaching and learning with the founding of the Faculty Center for Teaching and Learning, Campus Writing and Speaking Program, and Serving Learning Program; formation of the Standing Committee on the Evaluation of Teaching; the work of

CUE and Council on Undergraduate Program Review; and adoption of individual and department teaching awards

Subsequent Actions in IGL

Several major projects and programs that made up the inquiry-guided learning initiative were initiated by faculty (see Table 1). Participation in any of the projects and programs required integration of inquiry-guided learning into one or more courses taught by an individual faculty member or a sequence of courses in the major taught by several instructors in an academic department and subsequent assessment of the effectiveness of the integration.

Each project or program also supplied various forms of support to assist participating faculty members as they transformed their courses through introduction of inquiry-guided learning. The types of support varied somewhat from project to project but generally included in-house workshops on inquiry-guided learning and its assessment, individual consultations, peer observation of teaching, weekend retreats often facilitated by an outside consultant, informal gatherings sometimes at a faculty member's home, campuswide symposia on inquiry-guided learning, opportunities for faculty to participate in conferences and national projects, and financial support for wider dissemination of IGL in the department.

As was already noted, our shared understanding of inquiry-guided learning was sufficiently broad that faculty members had significant discretion in how they integrated inquiry-guided learning in their courses. The degree of integration varied from one faculty member to the next, depending on a variety of factors, among them academic discipline, faculty rank, support from the academic department for the instructor's participation in the project, prior assumptions about teaching and learning, and the instructor's comfort level with active learning on entering.

Overall Findings

In a large research university such as NC State, undergraduate education reform on the scale originally imagined through the inquiry-guided learning initiative is extremely challenging because of the varied sources of resistance within the institution. Taking the IGL initiative as a whole, we experimented with three broad areas of assessment: faculty learning, student learning, and (to a far lesser extent) institutional learning, by which we mean the capacity of the institution as a whole to change its structures and policies over time in ways that support intended student learning outcomes. Despite a culture of assessment at NC State, getting faculty buy-in for assessment was challenging. When we got buy-in, our findings were at once elusive and inconclusive, but suggestive of qualified success.

New Directions for Teaching and Learning • DOI: 10.1002/tl

Table 1. Inquiry-Guided Learning at North Carolina State University: Major Initiatives

Dates	Program Title	Participating Units	Focus	Program Features	Assessment
<1997	Independent Faculty Initiatives CUE Report CUE Position Statement Richard Paul Workshop	Individual faculty Faculty senate CUE Div. of Undergraduate Affairs	Early exploration		
1997–1999	**Hewlett I** ($150,000, funded by Hewlett Foundation)	Individual faculty, staff, and graduate students (50) Div. of Undergraduate Affairs	Exploration of inquiry-guided learning with classroom experimentation in general education courses	Self-directed faculty groups Retreats and workshops with external facilitators	Quantitative study with comparison group
1999–2002	**First-Year Inquiry Courses** (2001–02, ~$271,000, funded by Div. of Undergraduate Affairs)	Sections: 1999–2000 (10); 2000–01 (28); 2001–02 (~46) Div. of Undergraduate Affairs	Small seminars for first-year students taught with inquiry-guided learning	Small classes (i.e., 20 students) Faculty development	Pre- and postessays assessed using Facione & Facione holistic critical thinking rubric; student self-report

2000–2001	**Hewlett Continuation** ($59,500, funded by NCSU Office of the Provost)	Individual faculty, staff, and graduate students (40) Hewlett Steering Committee Faculty Center for Teaching and Learning	Integration of inquiry-guided learning in individual courses	Outcomes-based course development process Common understanding of inquiry-guided learning Resource handbook Retreats and workshops with external or internal facilitators Small working groups Campuswide dissemination	Faculty self-report and external assessment
2000–2003	**Hewlett Campus Challenge** ($150,000, funded by Hewlett Foundation)	Departmental teams (10) Faculty Center for Teaching and Learning Campus Writing and Speaking Program Div. of Undergraduate Affairs University Planning and Analysis	Institutionalization of inquiry-guided learning in the departmental major with multiunit collaboration	Outcomes-based course and curriculum planning Orchestration of campus initiatives Resource handbook Retreats and workshops with external or internal facilitators Departmental and campuswide dissemination	Program assessment using program review and assessment process

By far the most compelling finding concerned faculty learning. Across the programs and projects in the initiative, both instructors and students reported changes in classroom practices consistent with inquiry-guided learning. Two outside evaluators from Alverno College also noted changes comparable to those reported by instructors and students. These practices include interpreting the broad IGL student learning outcomes in terms of more specific goals and objectives for their courses, identifying and implementing strategies to help students become more active learners, and beginning to design assignments that required students to perform in ways that would demonstrate the ability to think critically and inquire within the discipline. Equally encouraging if not more so, instructors were excited about the changes they were making in their courses and by the heightened level of student engagement in their courses. Finally, in one early study student ratings of their instructors' teaching style were significantly higher on basic skills, inquiry-guided instruction, and Bloom's taxonomy (classroom environment conducted at higher levels of the taxonomy) than in the comparison group (Lindblad, 2001).

Instructors reported anecdotally on promising changes in student behavior (better attendance, increased participation and more positive affect, increased student self-confidence, better quality student work), but demonstrating actual changes in student learning that were due to IGL practices was challenging. Part of the difficulty lay in engaging instructors in course-based assessment with the antecedent requirement that they plan their courses intentionally and consistently using intended learning outcomes. For several years, the First Year Inquiry Program collected a random sample of early- and late-semester essays designed to assess students' ability to think critically. A small group of specially trained faculty members from the program rated the essays using a holistic critical-thinking rubric. From this assessment, there appeared to be no significant change in students' critical-thinking ability. However, the exercise was tremendously useful from a faculty development standpoint, raising many important questions about assignment and rubric design, timing of developmental changes in complex abilities, and more. In the second Hewlett-funded project, departments designed their own assessments within the requirements of the program review process. These assessments yielded some evidence of patterns of student learning in selected courses that the departments used to modify instructional approaches, ranging from laboratory design to textbook selection (Lee, 2004a).

Increasingly we recognized that the ultimate success of the IGL initiative as an institutionwide reform effort depended on fundamental changes in organizational structures and policies as well as allocation of resources. For example, in most cases untenured faculty members who invested a significant amount of time in their teaching did so at their peril, given the existing requirements for tenure. Even among the tenured faculty, reaching successive tiers of instructors beyond the early adopters seemed to depend, in large part, on external and enduring incentives for making changes in their teaching consistent with inquiry-guided learning. The comparative success of isolated departments in the second Hewlett-funded project permitted important insights on conditions within the academic department that supported reform (Lee, Hyman, & Luginbuhl, 2007). Further, two on-campus institutes on inquiry-guided learning brought together selected participants across the four IGL projects and programs to share effective practices. Both institutes were promising vehicles for (1) bridging the natural boundaries of the university and the isolated warrens of undergraduate experience within those boundaries, (2) consolidating learning about best practice and moving practice forward collectively, and (3) at least beginning to visualize a new trajectory of undergraduate experience across general education and the major.

Lessons Learned

Several themes have emerged in considering what has happened to the IGL initiative in the years since completion of the second Hewlett-funded project in 2003. In programs in which IGL approaches were part of elective courses in a core curriculum, maintaining, if not increasing, the commitment to IGL within a department or curriculum requires at least one champion among the faculty, someone who is always there to keep the interest alive. For example, monthly meetings of instructors teaching a set of courses in which IGL issues were regularly discussed did not survive the sabbatical of the individual who had originally organized them. In other departments, changing faculty assignments and hiring new instructors, especially in courses with more than one section, contributed to dilution of the original enthusiasm.

By contrast, a program in which all faculty involved from the outset remained in place has continued to expand its use of IGL, such that students now experience some form of inquiry-guided learning in almost all of their courses from freshman through senior year. In addition, IGL principles have remained strong in a program that was created *de novo* as part of the initiative.

Another theme involves student response to IGL. Replacing traditional lectures with active classroom and laboratory activities has become a hook that one department uses to attract new students to, and retain them in, its curriculum. As noted by one of its professors, the IGL tenet that students take responsibility for their own learning has facilitated a gradual shift toward more frequent presentation of basic concepts in online teaching modules that must be watched prior to class, allowing class time to be spent applying those principles to group problem-solving activities. When given the option of having to spend several hours preparing for class, with the promise of being challenged once they get there with issues that they find engaging, most students in this program seem willing to accept the extra work.

Still, semester-by-semester differences in the student population in small classes can dramatically alter the experience. One faculty member spent an entire semester worrying that his previous successful use of IGL was a fluke, only to discover in the next two years that it was the students in that semester who were unusual. However, it is clear that when IGL is focused on only one course in a curriculum (rather than a programwide paradigm), it can take a while for students to accept its approach. Even in IGL-infused curricula, instructors must help students unlearn the habits of mind they have developed in any prerequisite courses that were taken in other departments. Interestingly, one instructor finds that it is often the students with higher GPAs who resist the approach the most. Because they have always been successful in the traditional classroom environment, it can be harder for them to accept such a significant change in their approach to learning.

Interpretation of "student responsibility" as meaning an expectation that more time is spent out of class learning the basics, or in some cases reviewing the basics, appears to be a strong driver of continued curriculum and course transformation for several individual faculty members as well as programs, especially those that need to ensure mastery of content but are also preparing students for jobs within their profession immediately upon graduation. Technology has clearly made this easier because typical lecture content can be moved online. Although this requires more time up front for instructors to create the material, they find that time spent on actual classroom preparation during the semester decreases significantly.

Even though individual faculty members within a group may not have maintained their interest, changes in the physical environment as a result of the original IGL initiative have left a permanent legacy that facilitates its adoption by others. In fact, the design of classrooms and common space in a new campus building was largely informed by the desire to create constant opportunities for student inquiry: movable tables and chairs in classrooms surrounded by white boards, and common areas where students and faculty can mingle, again having white boards within reach.

A recent qualitative study of the faculty participants in the campuswide First Year Inquiry program (McClure, Atkinson, & Wills, 2008) found that training in IGL principles for the freshman seminars resulted in a "positive transfer effect" to faculty members' other courses (large and small), both in the major as well as in the general education curriculum. In addition, being a member of a community of practice has enhanced support for engaging in the scholarship of teaching and learning, an important way for faculty in tenure track positions to justify time spent on teaching. First Year Inquiry instructors have published or have in press nine papers in peer-reviewed journals on their use of IGL.

Unfortunately, the current budget shortfall has resulted in suspension of the First Year Inquiry program. But in recognition of the financial challenges associated with maintaining small class sizes at a large public research university, another initiative, involving current and former faculty FYI participants, has led to a National Science Foundation grant proposal requesting funds to develop larger IGL-based courses. This request also stems from changes in our general education program, which now includes a five-credit-hour requirement in an *interdisciplinary perspectives* (IP) category. The proposal follows the successful FYI faculty development model, with the goal of integrating interdisciplinary STEM teaching and learning into the general education curriculum through piloting of a large-scale freshman course. Because the IP category can be met by courses within the major, the proposal also includes development of a senior-level capstone course. In this way, the proposal seeks to expand on the intent of the original grant in 1996 that began our IGL journey: to incorporate principles of critical thinking and student responsibility for learning across the entire curriculum, from freshman to senior year, from general education courses to courses in the major.

References

Blanchard, S., Bresciani, M., Carter, M., Lee, V. S., & Luginbuhl, G. (2004). Inquiry-guided learning and the undergraduate curriculum: General education and the major. In V. S. Lee (Ed.), *Teaching and learning through inquiry: A guidebook for institutions and instructors* (pp. 183–204). Sterling, VA: Stylus.

Greene, D. B., Lee, V. S., & Wellman, J. D. (2004). Inquiry-guided learning at North Carolina State University: A brief history. In V. S. Lee (Ed.), *Teaching and learning through inquiry: A guidebook for institutions and instructors* (pp. 17–28). Sterling, VA: Stylus.

Hewlett Steering Committee. (2004). What is inquiry-guided learning? In V. S. Lee (Ed.), *Teaching and learning through inquiry: A guidebook for institutions and instructors* (pp. 9–10). Sterling, VA: Stylus.

Lee, V. S. (2004a). Assessing the impact of inquiry-guided learning at NCSU. In V. S. Lee (Ed.), *Teaching and learning through inquiry: A guidebook for institutions and instructors* (pp. 259–275). Sterling, VA: Stylus.

Lee, V. S. (Ed.). (2004b). *Teaching and learning through inquiry: A guidebook for institutions and instructors.* Sterling, VA: Stylus.

Lee, V. S., Hyman, M., & Luginbuhl, G. (2007). The concept of readiness in the academic department: A case study of undergraduate education reform. *Innovative Higher Education, 32*(1), 3–18.

Lindblad, M. (2001). *Internal analysis of the Hewlett I project.* Raleigh, NC: North Carolina State University.

McClure, A. L., Atkinson, M. P., & Wills, J. B. (2008). Transferring teaching skills: Faculty development effects from a first year inquiry program. *Journal of the First-Year Experience & Students in Transition, 20*, 31–52.

NC State University Council on Undergraduate Education (2004). Position statement on increasing student responsibility for, involvement in and commitment to learning. In V. S. Lee (Ed.), *Teaching and learning through inquiry: A guidebook for institutions and instructors* (pp. 191–193). Sterling, VA: Stylus.

VIRGINIA S. LEE *is principal and senior consultant of Virginia S. Lee & Associates, a consulting firm specializing in teaching, learning and assessment in higher education. Previously she was associate director, Faculty Center for Teaching and Learning at North Carolina State University, and director, Graduate Student Teaching Programs, and consultant, Center for Teaching and Learning, UNC-Chapel Hill. She held visiting faculty appointments at both universities. She is a former president of the Professional and Organizational Development (POD) Network in Higher Education, the largest faculty development professional organization in North America. She earned her Ph.D. in Educational Psychology from UNC-Chapel Hill.*

SARAH ASH *is an associate professor in the Department of Food, Bioprocessing, and Nutrition Sciences, and the coordinator of the undergraduate Nutrition Program. She teaches over 1,000 students a year in a wide variety of classes, from introductory nutrition to U.S. food history. Her scholarly work examines best practices in critical reflection associated with applied learning pedagogies. She is the recipient of numerous teaching awards including the NCSU Alumni Distinguished Professor Award and the USDA Food and Agriculture Sciences Excellence in Teaching Award. She earned an A.B. degree in Biology from Harvard University, and M.S. and Ph.D. degrees in Nutrition from Tufts University.*

NEW DIRECTIONS FOR TEACHING AND LEARNING • DOI: 10.1002/tl

5

*University of the Pacific is a private, comprehensive
university with a College of Arts and Sciences and six
professional schools, and with a population of more than
four thousand students on its main campus in the ethnically diverse central valley city of Stockton, California.
The signature component of Pacific's general education
program is the required three Pacific Seminars (PACS)
that focus on the question "What is a Good Society?"
PACS 1 and 2 are writing-intensive, discussion-oriented
seminars taken in sequence in the first year, and each
course consists of some forty sections of about twenty
students per section. PACS 3 is a culminating educational
experience taken in the senior year and consists of thirty-
one sections of twenty-five students per section spread
throughout the entire year.*

University of the Pacific's Bookend Seminars on a Good Society

Lou Matz

Students at University of the Pacific engage the question of a good society
in a series of three discussion-oriented seminars that prepare them for a life-
time of self-reflection and active citizenship. University of the Pacific is a
private, comprehensive university located in the ethnically diverse Central
Valley city of Stockton, California. There is a College of Arts and Sciences
and six professional schools with a population of more than four thousand
students. Pacific's general education program is composed of three required
"Pacific Seminars" and a nine-area breadth program. The nine areas of the
breadth program are individual and interpersonal behavior; U.S. studies;
global studies; language and literature; worldviews and ethics; visual and
performing arts; natural science, with a lab component; mathematics
and formal logic; and science, technology, and society. The three Pacific
Seminars (PACS) focus on the question, "What is a Good Society?" and are
taught by faculty from every school and every department in the College of
Arts and Sciences. PACS 1 and 2 are taken in sequence in the first year, and

I would like to thank Catherine Wehlburg and Cynthia Dobbs for their valuable comments on earlier drafts of this article.

NEW DIRECTIONS FOR TEACHING AND LEARNING, no. 121, Spring 2010 © Wiley Periodicals, Inc.
Published online in Wiley InterScience (www.interscience.wiley.com) • DOI: 10.1002/tl.387

47

PACS 3 is taken in the senior year. PACS 1 introduces students to the question of a good society by examining a range of issues, and PACS 2 explores a theme or themes from PACS 1 in greater depth. PACS 3 is taken in the senior year and focuses on ethics and students' own ethical autobiographies. The Pacific Seminars thus form a common core experience within the broader general education program. The core is concentrated in the students' critical first year and returns in the senior year so they can reflect on their ethical identity as they enter the world beyond the university.

The Pacific Seminars

PACS 1 introduces students to the question of a good society through a shared intellectual experience based on a faculty-edited course reader and a common syllabus. The course reader is divided into five chapters, which progress from personal and local realms to more public and universal realms: the self and self-reflection; family and interpersonal relationships; the institutions of civil society; citizenship and the state; and the natural world and the environment. Each chapter includes both historical and contemporary readings on a number of specific issues. The principal goals of PACS 1 are to promote critical self-reflection on significant personal, social, and political issues through extensive writing, careful reading, and seminar-style class discussion. The common assignments include three formal essays as well as additional writing assignments. Although there are guidelines for these assignments, faculty have the autonomy to create the formal essay topics and types of additional writing assignments. As intentional writing-intensive courses, PACS 1 and PACS 2 constitute Pacific's university-level writing requirement (students are not required to take a traditional English composition course). By the end of the semester, students are required to post their best written work and self-reflection on it in an electronic portfolio that will be carried through to PACS 2.

In PACS 2, students choose from more than forty topical seminars that examine one or more of the five broad chapter themes from PACS 1. These seminars are offered in almost every school and virtually every department in the College of Arts and Sciences and are some of the most innovative courses at Pacific. Some seminar titles follow: "And Justice for All," "Gaia's Got a Fever," "Imagine There's No Countries," "The Pursuit of Happiness," "Economics and Social Welfare," "Mass Media and Popular Culture," "Drama and Community," "Mathematics and Social Issues," "The Role of Business in Society," "Animal Rights and Wrongs," and "Divided by Faith." Although faculty have the autonomy to create the content and assignments in the course, there are common course guidelines and expectations, including a minimum of twenty formal written pages, a scholarly research project (which counts as part of the twenty pages), and a formal oral presentation. Faculty are encouraged to assign at least one reading in the course from the PACS 1 anthology in order to connect the seminars more explicitly. Furthermore, several sections include some form of experiential learning such as a field trip or hours of community-based learning. Students in all sections continue developing their e-portfolio by posting their research project and corresponding self-reflection statement.

In their senior year, students from all majors come together again in PACS 3, a culminating educational experience that develops students' capacity for ethical self-understanding and ethical reasoning, primarily through various forms of narrative assignments. From a common course reader edited by Pacific faculty, students learn about moral development theories and ethical theories, and they examine a number of perspectives on ethical issues in the realms of family, friends, work, and citizenship—themes that intentionally refer back to PACS 1 and 2. However, unlike PACS 1, there is no uniform reading schedule in PACS 3; rather, faculty must devote a specified minimum amount of class time to address certain required course themes: moral development theory; ethical theories (such as utilitarianism, Kantianism, and virtue ethics theory); philosophical issues such as ethical relativism, the relationship between ethics and religion, and altruism and egoism; and issues regarding family and friendship, work, and citizenship. There are some common course assignments, including the centerpiece assignment in which students apply the theoretical material of the course to their own lives by writing an ethical autobiography. Students also complete a "narrative" assignment where they read a biography or work of literature of ethical significance.

The Pacific Seminars' course objectives and required course assignments are listed in Table 1.

The Pacific Seminars collectively incorporate six of the ten high-impact educational practices that empirical research in higher education has shown to be most effective: first-year seminars, common intellectual experiences, learning communities, writing-intensive courses, diversity and global learning, and capstone courses (Kuh, 2008). Moreover, the essential learning outcomes in PACS 1 and 2 reflect virtually all of the proposed universitywide learning objectives (critical and creative thinking, communication, intercultural and global perspectives, ethical reasoning, sustainability, and collaboration and leadership; see the Appendix for their corresponding indicators), thereby establishing a firm foundation for their future development in major, general education, and elective courses. The seminars are thus rightly emphasized to prospective students as a distinctive and foundational aspect of the Pacific experience.

Origin of the Pacific Seminars

Prior to 1992, Pacific used an exclusively "menu-based" approach to general education; students completed one course from many options in twelve different content areas. An impending accreditation visit prompted Pacific to revise its general education program. As a result of extensive faculty collaboration, a nine-area breadth program was retained from the previous

Table 1. Pacific Seminar Course Objectives and Assignments

Course	Course Objectives	Required Course Assignments
PACS 1	1. Examine and expand one's assumptions and beliefs about a good society. 2. Develop and understand the process of critical thinking through reading, writing, and class discussion. 3. Reflect on one's personal and social responsibilities. 4. Recognize the value of intellectual curiosity and lifelong learning.	Three formal essays (4–5 pages) Additional writing assignments Class discussion
PACS 2	1. Continue the study of the question, "What is a Good Society?" from Pacific Seminar 1 through a discipline-specific perspective. 2. Develop academic writing and research skills appropriate to lower-level freshman students within a writing-intensive course. 3. Develop critical thinking and oral presentation skills. 4. Broaden social awareness and encourage engaged citizenship.	Twenty pages of formal writing, which includes a research project that is a minimum of seven pages Additional informal writing Oral presentation Class discussion
PACS 3	1. Identify, analyze, and evaluate one's own moral values and framework(s). 2. Understand moral development theories and apply them to one's own moral development. 3. Understand and apply moral theories to one's life and to analysis of contemporary issues regarding family, friends, work, and citizenship. 4. Understand how narrative can illuminate moral development and experience as applied to oneself and others.	Ethical autobiography Narrative assignment Exam, essay, or comparable assignment Class discussion

twelve-area menu, and three new "mentor seminars" were created to form a core intellectual experience for students and for faculty. The mentor seminars had strong support from many senior faculty members, who became leaders in the program. Mentor I was taken in the first semester, with a common reader and syllabus, and focused on "timeless" questions such as the nature of knowledge; the origin of the universe and human life; issues regarding race, gender, and sexuality; and the nature of the good life. Mentor II was taken in the second semester and focused on contemporary social problems. Students learned to do academic research by writing a substantial group policy paper in small groups, and they presented their research in an all-course oral presentation competition. In later years, students could enroll in community-based learning sections of Mentor II, and at its height almost half of the sections were community-based learning ones. Mentor III was eventually implemented in 1994 as a capstone experience related to general education. This course was taken in the junior or senior year and focused on the ethical implications of knowledge. The centerpiece assignments were the ethical autobiography and a biography project and presentation. Over time, some professional schools and departments in the College of Arts and Sciences developed their own specialized Mentor III sections for their majors.

The mentor seminars were successful in many ways, and for years they had substantial faculty commitment. However, by the time of the 2003 general education program review, many of the faculty who founded and taught in the program had retired, and there was a growing lack of faculty commitment to the seminars, especially to Mentor I and II, for two main reasons: the courses were demanding to teach in terms of both content (they were on topics outside of faculty expertise) and method (they were discussion-oriented and writing-intensive), and the courses detracted from work that really counted for tenure and promotion.

After the program review, a survey was sent to faculty to identify new directions for the general education program. On the basis of survey results, the general education director formed a committee to revise the mentor seminars. This committee recommended that all three seminars be unified by the common theme, "What is a Good Society?" and that the first-semester course continue to have a uniform format but that the second-semester course be composed of different topical seminars rooted in the areas of faculty expertise and interest. The planning committee anticipated that these changes would have some advantages over the mentor seminars: revitalization of faculty commitment to the first-year seminars, a direct thematic connection among all of the seminars through the shared focus on the issue of a good society, more interdisciplinary contact in the first-year seminars, enhanced ability to assess the program, strengthening of the quality of the scholarly research project in the new PACS 2 course, and, finally, a nationally distinctive structure to the first-year experience, based on data from the National Research Council (see http://www.sc.edu/fye/research/index.html). The three Pacific Seminars were officially launched in 2006–07.

Pacific Seminar Campus Collaboration

A long-standing collaboration between the Office of Student Life and the first-year mentor seminars as well as between the library and the Mentor Seminar II course existed throughout the history of the seminars. After installment of the Pacific seminars, these collaborations were strengthened and extended to other campus constituencies, such as the Office of Institutional Research, the Office of Institutional Technology, the Departments of Visual Arts and Communication, and the Career Resource Center. In PACS 1, there are now eighteen PACS 1 Residential Learning Community

NEW DIRECTIONS FOR TEACHING AND LEARNING • DOI: 10.1002/tl

sections (RLCs). Students from the same residential hall are placed in sections in order to foster a living-learning environment. Learning activities in the residence halls over the past few years have included newspaper boards with articles relevant to the course readings and themes, study sessions, and public showings of the two PACS 1 films. In PACS 2, a required, hands-on tutorial in the library was established in 2007. A library liaison is assigned to each section and tailors the session to help faculty instruct students on how to conduct scholarly research in their respective thematic areas. Although there are no residential learning communities in PACS 2, faculty have given a number of informal talks in residence halls on issues in their PACS 2 courses.

In fall 2008, the role of student advisors was expanded to support the goals of PACS 1 and 2. Student advisors are directed through the Office of Student Life and have traditionally been responsible for guiding their group of first-year students through the first year at Pacific as well as providing some support for faculty advisors during orientation. Student advisors now meet with their group of students a few times in both semesters to reinforce the nature of academic expectations, emphasize the nature and value of academic integrity, and help students with their e-portfolios as well as monitor their required postings to it.

The Pacific seminar program has also collaborated for years with the Center for Teaching and Learning to train faculty to use a course management system to enhance the teaching and learning experience. An anticipated consequence of this course management system requirement was that its use would spread to the faculty's other courses and to faculty who did not teach in the program. Moreover, other faculty development activities, such as teaching writing or using active teaching techniques, reach all of the schools and thus create shared teaching practices and foster ongoing discussion about their improvement.

For the past several years, the three Cooperative Institutional Research Program (CIRP) surveys have been administered during class in each of the Pacific Seminars: the Freshman Survey in PACS 1, Your First College Year (YFCY) Survey in PACS 2, and the College Senior survey in PACS 3. This mode of administration ensures a high response rate for collection of this important institutional data. It also gives the faculty an opportunity to learn more about our students. The director of general education worked with the director of institutional research to identify those questions from the freshman CIRP that are most relevant for PACS 1: students' self-ratings on their various abilities, their reasons for going to college, and their moral and political opinions that connect to issues in the course. The CIRP results are posted on the PACS 1 faculty organization site in the course management system, and faculty are encouraged to review them and make reference to them during the course. Finally, since 2006, Pacific undergraduates, via an assignment and competition in a graphic design course, have designed the covers for the faculty-edited PACS 1 and PACS 3 readers. Students receive information about the PACS courses in advance (most have taken them) and then present their cover designs to a group of faculty who choose the winners. This collaboration is just one example of the student-centered focus at Pacific.

Faculty Development

The quality of the Pacific Seminars depends on regular faculty development, and there have been a variety of faculty development activities. There are frequent faculty meetings in PACS 1 to discuss all aspects of the course, such as ideas on active teaching techniques for the specific readings, how to evaluate writing, and how to approach difficult situations. These meetings are supplemented by posting teaching ideas on the all-faculty course management site. Though less regular, there are also PACS 2 and 3 faculty meetings and corresponding supplemental use of the all-faculty course management site to post teaching ideas and sample course syllabi. There are faculty planning committees for each of the Pacific Seminars, which reevaluate the course every year according to student and faculty feedback. These committees also determine the nature and frequency of the faculty meetings and the kinds of faculty development activities that are most needed. The PACS 1 planning committee is the most challenging; it revises the course reader every year and must negotiate inevitable disagreements about the pace of the course as well as the kinds of readings that should be included. For PACS 1 faculty, there have been additional, frequent formal workshops to discuss how to teach writing, and faculty receive reference materials and other documents. In 2007, PACS 1 faculty were formally trained in the use of the Kolb Learning Style Inventory (LSI) in order to expand their teaching styles and discuss their students' results on the LSI, which was administered in all of the PACS 1 sections (Kolb, 1984).

As a result of Pacific's 2007–2009 AAC&U Core Commitments Leadership Consortium membership, there have been additional faculty development workshops. These workshops have included trainings on understanding and advancing students' cognitive development in college, and trainings for PACS 3 faculty on how to improve the teaching of moral development theory as well as reorienting faculty to teaching the course.

Finally, the general education director works closely with the director of the Center for Teaching and Learning (CTL) to create an additional layer of faculty development support. The director of CTL has made various presentations at the PACS faculty meetings, such as using technology and development and use of rubrics, and has attended planning committee meetings to contribute ideas to course design.

Assessment of Student Learning in the PACS

There has not yet been any direct formal assessment of student learning in the Pacific seminar program as a whole. With establishment of the PACS program, the general education committee decided to implement an electronic portfolio that could assess student learning at various junctures, such as at the end of the first year in PACS 2 or in the senior year. An ad hoc e-portfolio committee was formed—which included faculty, assessment specialists, and the vice president and dean of student life—to identify the five most essential general education objectives and their indicators. The committee chose written communication, critical thinking, ethics and civic engagement, intercultural awareness and interaction, and leadership. Aside from their role in assessment, the e-portfolio would serve other purposes, such as helping students integrate the learning in their coursework and their activities outside of class, giving students a structured opportunity to make connections among seemingly unrelated courses and activities, providing an archive of self-reflection on their learning that could be used for their ethical autobiography in PACS 3, and using selected work from their portfolio for employment and internship applications. By fall 2007, the first-year class was formally trained on the learning goals and how to create an e-portfolio. Students were required to post their best written work in the written communication outcome in both PACS 1 and PACS 2. These required postings in the first year are the first step in doing direct assessment of the impact of PACS 1 and 2. However, such assessment has not yet happened, mostly because of a lack of staff support to implement it.

At this time, then, we have only self-reported student data on their perceived gains in the PACS courses (see Tables 2, 3, and 4) and the feedback of the PACS faculty on their students' learning. One noteworthy aspect in student evaluations of the three seminars is the importance of the discussion-oriented class sessions in advancing their learning.

Sustainability of the Pacific Seminars

The Pacific Seminars have attracted national visibility through the Association of American Colleges and Universities (AAC&U). They were the foundation of Pacific's successful proposal for the AAC&U Core Commitments

Table 2. 2007 and 2008 PACS 1 Mean Student Self-Ratings in All Sections

Course Elements from Which Most Learning Occurred	Most Developed Skills as a Result of the Course
Class meetings (4.2)	Critical thinking (4.0)
Course readings (3.8)	Social and political awareness (4.0)
Formal essays (3.7)	Interest to be an involved citizen (3.9)
Additional writing (3.4)	Discussion (3.8)
Peer review of essays (3.3)	Writing (3.7)

Note: "1" is the lowest and "5" the highest.

Table 3. 2008 and 2009 PACS 2 Mean Student Self-Ratings in All Sections

Course Elements from Which Most Learning Occurred	Most Developed Skills as a Result of the Course
Class meetings (4.2)	Research (4.1)
Research project (4.1)	Social and political awareness (4.0)
Course readings (3.9)	Critical thinking (3.9)
Oral presentations (3.8)	Interest to be an involved citizen (3.8)
	Writing (3.7)

Note: "1" is the lowest and "5" the highest.

Leadership Consortium, whose purpose was to lead a national conversation about making personal and social responsibility an essential learning goal in higher education. Pacific was also one of eleven universities to be selected by AAC&U to produce a video on best educational practices that aired at the 2008 annual AAC&U meeting, and the video was on the Pacific Seminars. Finally, there have been many presentations about the Pacific seminars at AAC&U annual and academic renewal meetings, and at the annual National Resource Center Conference on the First-Year Experience. The seminars appear to have much more faculty support than they did at the end of the mentor seminar era, and student satisfaction with the courses and instruction has been generally good.

Nonetheless, the structure, incentives, and size of the program have created some ongoing difficulties. The PACS 2 seminars have understandably reinvested a number faculty in the program, and although the theme of PACS 1 has broadened its appeal to faculty the common course design and writing-intensive nature make it nonetheless too challenging for some faculty. To be sure, there are benefits for faculty who teach PACS 1; faculty

Table 4. 2008–09 PACS 3 Mean Student Self-Ratings in All Sections

Course Elements from Which Most Learning Occurred	Course Objectives Best Met
Class discussion (4.4)	Ability to identify, analyze, and evaluate my moral values (4.3)
Films (4.3)	
Autobiography (4.0)	Understanding ethical theories (4.3)
Narrative assignment (3.8)	Ability to apply ethical theories and concepts to my life (4.3)
Course reader (3.6)	
	Understanding moral development theories (4.2)

Note: "1" is the lowest and "5" the highest.

NEW DIRECTIONS FOR TEACHING AND LEARNING • DOI: 10.1002/tl

gain new ideas in the faculty meetings to improve their teaching, they can attract new students to their departmental courses, and full-time faculty who teach PACS 1 now receive a $1,000 research and travel award to recognize the commitment the course requires. However, any advantages in teaching in the program may be outweighed by the realities of promotion and tenure requirements, which privilege traditional scholarship and teaching in one's department or school. The cost of teaching in the PACS program, especially PACS 1, is thus not adequately rewarded in faculty evaluation, and it is not evenly shared among faculty.

Finally, the PACS program is now relying again on ever more part-time faculty, particularly in PACS 1. Although the part-time faculty have performed well and have been deeply committed to the program, it is problematic not to have more tenure-track and full-time faculty teaching in such a truly distinctive program; the percentage has gone from 72 percent tenure-track and full-time faculty teaching the PACS in 2007–08 to 61 percent in 2009–10. These structural problems are solvable, but they require the political will of the faculty, department chairs, deans, the provost, and the president to be met.

References

Kolb, D. (1984). *Experiential learning: Experience as the source of learning and development*. Upper Saddle River, NJ: Prentice Hall.

Kuh, G. (2008). *High-impact educational practices: What they are, who has access to them, and why they matter*. Washington, D.C.: Association for American Colleges and Universities.

Appendix: Pacific's Universitywide Objectives and Outcomes

Critical and Creative Thinking
  Apply reasoning and evidence to judge and support claims.
  Effectively analyze, integrate, and evaluate information.
  Construct well-reasoned arguments and solutions.
  Create novel approaches in a variety of contexts.
Communication
  Prepare and deliver effective forms of communication.
  Adapt communication style to the occasion, task, and audience.
  Select and use appropriate communication technologies.
Collaboration and Leadership
  Work cooperatively with others toward a common goal.
  Demonstrate effective social interaction skills appropriate to the occasion, task, and audience.
  Influence others ethically toward achievement of a common goal to effect positive change.
  Demonstrate accountability for one's decisions and actions.

Intercultural and Global Perspectives
  Articulate the broad set of influences that have shaped one's personal identity.
  Effectively and appropriately interact in a variety of cultural contexts.
  Explain the interdependence of nations and peoples.
  Engage in the civic life of the local, national, and global community.
Ethical Reasoning
  Articulate one's own ethical beliefs and their origins.
  Identify ethical issues in personal, professional, and civic life.
  Evaluate assumptions and implications of various ethical perspectives.
  Defend ethical positions with reason, and consider alternative courses of action.
Sustainability
  Identify the interconnectedness between humans and their natural environment.
  Evaluate the social, economic, and environmental consequences of individual and group actions.
  Engage in responsible environmental action.

LOU MATZ is an associate professor of Philosophy and the associate dean and director of General Education at University of the Pacific. He led the revision of Pacific's general education program and has been involved with the Association of American Colleges and Universities (AAC&U) as Pacific's team leader in Core Commitments and as a member of the VALUE project. Prior to his administrative appointment, he taught philosophy at Pacific, Xavier University (Ohio), University of California, San Diego, and the University of Redlands. His research interests focus on the philosophy of religion, particularly J.S. Mill, and ethics. He produced the first annotated edition of J.S. Mill's Three Essays on Religion (Broadview Press, 2009). He completed his M.A. and Ph.D. in philosophy at the University of California, San Diego.

NEW DIRECTIONS FOR TEACHING AND LEARNING • DOI: 10.1002/tl

6

In this chapter, the authors describe how faculty at Texas Christian University revised the institution's general education curriculum, discuss the design of the revised curriculum, explain the importance of the course vetting process to success of the implementation process, and discuss the assessment process.

Core Curriculum Revision at TCU: How Faculty Created and Are Maintaining the TCU Core Curriculum

Edward McNertney, Blaise Ferrandino

The initiative to revise Texas Christian University's (TCU) general education curriculum was one of the outcomes of an institutional strategic planning process in 2000, the Commission on the Future of TCU. Coincident with this planning process, TCU developed a new institutional mission statement that focused on preparing students for becoming responsible citizens and ethical leaders in the global community. The institution was then faced with the problem of designing a curriculum that would be consistent with the new mission statement and would facilitate assessment within the framework of the already existing academic structure of the university. To design such a curriculum would entail addressing the issues of how to match the goals of general education with the institution's mission and values, and how to meld general education with the students' major fields of study.

The first efforts to revise the core resulted in a faculty assembly meeting in January 2002, at which faculty expressed discontent with the proposed revision. The discontent came from problems with the process as much as with the proposed revision. Several committees had worked on the revision, and the resulting design was presented as a fait accompli. After listening to the comments at the faculty assembly, the chancellor asked the faculty senate to take over the process of designing a new core curriculum. The senate held a number of meetings throughout the spring semester to talk

New Directions for Teaching and Learning, no. 121, Spring 2010 © Wiley Periodicals, Inc.
Published online in Wiley InterScience (www.interscience.wiley.com) • DOI: 10.1002/tl.388

with faculty regarding the revision process and offered the skeleton of a design by the end of the semester. At its last meeting of the academic year, the senate voted to set up an ad hoc Core Curriculum Committee (CCC) to finish the design and write the competencies and student learning outcomes. The senate elected CCC members in September 2002 and the committee began deliberations the same month.

The curricular reform process was guided by three overarching goals:

1. Faculty, in a broadly participatory process, must design the TCU Core Curriculum.
2. The TCU Core Curriculum must embody the mission of the university.
3. The TCU Core Curriculum must be explicitly designed to incorporate student-learning outcomes.

In addition, the CCC recommended that the result of the committee's work be taken to the faculty senate for a vote of approval or disapproval and, if approved, to the faculty assembly for a similar vote. It was later decided that the faculty senate and assembly should also have the opportunity to approve or disapprove the competencies and learning outcomes for each of the core categories. These process decisions wound up being crucial to gaining faculty support for the revised core because faculty became very involved in the revision process. For example, the social science and humanities competencies, written by faculty from departments in those areas, were presented to the social science and humanities faculty at a college meeting, and then, after discussion, revision, and approval, were taken to the faculty senate for review. A similar procedure was followed for other core categories.

TCU's General Education Curriculum

The faculty on the Core Curriculum Committee came from disciplines across the university and approached the task from the perspective of aligning the general education curriculum with the mission, vision, and values of the university. Because we were not specialists in curriculum design, we did not seek to create a curriculum that fell into any particular model of general education curriculum. The result was a hybrid that has components of several of the types of general education curriculum found in the literature.

The Association of American Colleges and Universities (2009) lists six types of general education curriculum:

1. *Distribution model.* Students take courses in specified areas to meet the requirements.
2. *Core curriculum.* The curriculum is designed around a predetermined set of skills and knowledge, and students are usually required to take the same set of core courses.

NEW DIRECTIONS FOR TEACHING AND LEARNING • DOI: 10.1002/tl

3. *Common intellectual experience.* Close to a core curriculum but offers more flexibility. The student takes a set of required common courses or a vertically organized general education program that includes advanced integrative studies or required participation in a learning community.
4. *Thematic required courses.* Within the theme, students have a choice of one or more courses that have been approved to satisfy the requirement.
5. *Upper-level requirements.* Some of the general education requirements must be fulfilled by courses at the upper division (junior-senior) level to furnish a general education experience throughout the undergraduate years.
6. *Learning communities.* Classes are linked or clustered during an academic term, often around an interdisciplinary theme, and enroll a common cohort of students.

TCU's general education curriculum is a hybrid of the first five of these general education models. It has elements of a distribution model in that it requires courses in various traditional categories (humanities, social sciences, natural sciences, and fine arts). It has elements of a core curriculum model because there are a predetermined set of skills and knowledge (mathematical reasoning, written and oral communication) in the essential competencies requirements that, de facto, students obtain from a common set of courses. It has elements of a common intellectual experience in that there are specified outcomes for each category (although not specified courses) and students are required to take at least one course from each category. It is thematic in that some of the categories (cultural awareness, global awareness, and citizenship and social values) are structured around themes. Once again, although there are no required courses in the theme categories, there are competencies and student learning outcomes for those categories. Finally, there are upper-level requirements in that the writing emphasis courses must be junior- or senior-level courses. There are also upper-level courses in almost all of the categories, which enable departments to overlay degree requirements with core requirements. (See Allen, 2006; Kuh, 2008; and "What Are Learning Communities?" (Washington Center, n.d.), for further discussion of types of core curriculum.)

Design of the TCU Core Curriculum. The TCU Core Curriculum links curriculum requirements to TCU's heritage, mission, vision, and values; focuses on the liberal arts; strengthens the foundation; and facilitates focus on educational competencies, learning outcomes, and assessment.

TCU's mission, vision, and values are:

- Mission: to educate individuals to think and act as ethical leaders and responsible citizens in the global community.
- Vision: to create a world-class, values-centered university experience for our students.
- Values: TCU values academic achievement, personal freedom and integrity, the dignity and respect of the individual, and a heritage of inclusiveness, tolerance, and service.

The link between institutional philosophy and learning outcomes occurs in the heritage, mission, vision, and values portion of the core (eighteen hours). TCU's heritage is explored by way of study of religious traditions, historical traditions, and literary traditions. The link to TCU's mission, vision, and values occurs in the cultural awareness, global awareness, and citizenship and social values categories. The competencies and learning outcomes for these categories were written so that students would have an opportunity to study cultural phenomena, global issues, and the rights and responsibilities of citizenship and leadership by taking courses in disciplines from throughout the university.

The liberal arts ethos of TCU is stated clearly in the heritage, philosophy, and goals section of TCU's Handbook for Faculty and Staff (Texas Christian University, 2009):

> The University . . . regards as essential the advancement and communication of general knowledge which enables students to understand the past, to comprehend the natural and social order, to search for the good and the beautiful, and to integrate knowledge into significant wholes. [p. 1]

The focus on the liberal arts occurs in the human experiences and endeavors portion of the core (twenty-seven hours). Courses in this curriculum explore significant achievements and discoveries in the humanities, fine arts, social sciences, and natural sciences. The aim is to develop students' knowledge of the human condition and its connections to the good and the beautiful, and to the natural and social orders.

To prepare students for their other core and upper-level courses, it was necessary to build in a component that would strengthen their basic skills or essential competencies (twelve hours plus six hours of upper-division writing). Courses in this part of the curriculum are designed to establish a base of skills to ensure students' ability to communicate clearly and think analytically. Their focus is effective writing, mathematical reasoning, and oral communication.

The following summarizes the TCU core curriculum requirements:

- Human experiences and endeavors (HEE, twenty-seven hours)
- Heritage, mission, vision, and values (HMVV, eighteen hours)
- Essential competencies (EC, eighteen hours)

Therefore it appears that students must take sixty-three hours to complete the TCU Core Curriculum, leaving only sixty-one hours to complete the requirements of their major and minor. Although this would not pose much of a problem for students pursuing a degree in a discipline in liberal arts, it would be problematic for students in professional programs, some of which require seventy to eighty hours in the major. The university needed to be cognizant of the needs of these students as well as those in the more traditional liberal arts programs. The motivation for students seeking an advanced degree has changed, as seen in this quote: "The other reason for the growth of vocational majors is the marked increase in the number of students who look upon making money and succeeding in one's career as primary motivations for going to college. Since 1970, the percentage of freshmen who rate 'being very well off financially' as an 'essential' or 'very important' goal has risen from 36.2 to 73.6 percent, while the percentage who attach similar importance to 'acquiring a meaningful philosophy of life' has fallen from 79 to 39.6 percent" (Bok, 2006, p. 26).

This problem was solved by designing the core curriculum so that students can satisfy the requirements in a range of thirty-nine to sixty-three credit hours. The flexibility comes from what we have termed the overlay curriculum. Courses may be approved for one of the categories in the human experiences and endeavors curriculum and for one in the heritage, mission, vision, and values curriculum. Because of this design, a student could overlay the eighteen hours required for the HMVV curriculum with six courses (eighteen hours) approved for the HEE curriculum, thereby satisfying the forty-five-hour requirement with twenty-seven hours. In addition, writing emphasis courses may overlay with courses in the HEE and HMVV curriculums, thereby reducing the total by six more hours. It is also possible for core courses to overlay with other requirements of a student's degree program. This design promotes the flexibility needed to ensure a solid liberal arts education for all students without unduly lengthening the time period required to fulfill all discipline-specific degree requirements.

An integral part of the revision process was writing educational competencies and learning outcomes for each of the core categories. These are essential to effective curricular planning because they encompass pedagogical approach, assessment of student progress, faculty development, and subsequent revisions.

Course Vetting Process. The Core Curriculum Committee recommended, and the faculty senate approved, that courses must be vetted to become part of the core. In keeping with the spirit of educational learning outcomes, we thought it was essential for faculty to explain what students were going to do in their courses to achieve these competencies and learning outcomes. We carefully devised submission forms, field-tested them, and made revisions on the basis of initial submissions and comments. This turned out to be a marvelous faculty development opportunity, which was pointed out to us after several presentations we made at regional accreditation meetings.

The structure of the vetting process was important, but the methods used by the committees to vet the courses and to communicate the results of the committees' decisions to those submitting the courses were even more critical. We considered the process to be one of "revise and resubmit" and therefore carefully avoided "rejecting" any submissions (although some faculty may have thought we were doing so). Committee members called people on the phone, wrote careful letters, and met personally with many people individually and in groups. This careful approach helped create faculty buy-in to the revised core and good will.

Implementing and Managing the TCU Core Curriculum

The backing of academic support personnel was essential to the successful implementation and consequent management of the revised core. The registrar's office was the first office we brought into the discussions in spring 2004. After several meetings with the registrar, we jointly created a document, "New Core Implementation Assumptions," which offered guidance to all regarding some operational procedures.

The implementation process took a big step forward when an operational implementation group was created in January 2005. The associate provost for academic support suggested such a group and worked with the coordinator of the TCU Core Curriculum to compose it. The members included the registrar and associate registrars, associate deans of the colleges, staff from the deans' offices responsible for degree plans, the director of the Center for Academic Services, transfer credit analyst, representatives from the admissions office, and athletic academic advisors. The first meeting was a little contentious because some of the operational people were nervous about implementing the revised core. We first explained the requirements and then allowed them to express their concerns and ask questions. Gradually, we began to overcome the nervousness and move forward to a productive series of meetings. This was an important committee because it:

- Alleviated concerns
- Allowed colleges to begin to revise degree plans
- Allowed conversation between deans' offices and academic support personnel
- Gave academic support personnel a stake in the success of the revised core
- Let academic support personnel know they could influence operational policies

Assessment and Revision of the TCU Core Curriculum

The Core Implementation Committee recommended, and the faculty senate approved, a core assessment calendar that would require a "program review" of each core category every seven years.

Assessment. A review of the entire core will take place in the seventh year. The faculty senate "franchised" the responsibility to assess:

- College of Liberal Arts: humanities and social sciences
- College of Science and Engineering: natural sciences
- College of Fine Arts: fine arts
- Mathematics Department: mathematical reasoning
- Communication Studies Department: oral communication
- English Department: written communication 1 and 2

The directors of the Offices of Assessment and Quality Enhancement, Center for Teaching Excellence, and the TCU Core Curriculum created Faculty Learning Communities (FLCs) for the overlay categories. Two faculty were recruited to serve as cofacilitators of each FLC with the goals being to:

- Discuss teaching and learning issues and share pedagogy
- Talk about the methods faculty are using in their classes to help students attain the specified learning outcome(s)
- Help recruit new faculty and courses for the category
- Create parts of the review mechanism for the category
- Review data and discuss how to use the data in faculty development and curricular revision

The FLCs have taken on the task of assessing the HMVV categories. Their reports are delivered to the HMVV Committee for review (Wehlburg & McNertney, 2009).

The director of the TCU Core Committee asked the TCU Writing Committee to take on the task of vetting writing emphasis courses and serve as the assessment committee for writing emphasis.

Emendation and Course Information Policy. The 2003–04 Faculty Senate Executive Committee and the Core Implementation Committee felt it was essential to create a document that would specify the process by which the core could be revised in the future. The lack of such a document greatly hindered revision of the previous general education program, and we did not want to make the same mistake again. Therefore the Core Implementation Committee wrote an Emendation and Course Information Policy, which was approved by the faculty senate on January 27, 2005. The policy is divided into three major sections:

- Changes requiring only that the director of the core curriculum be notified, or given access to information, by the appropriate administrator or course instructor.
- Changes that must be approved by the appropriate unit, the director of the core curriculum, and the faculty senate executive committee.

- Changes that must be approved by the committee or person specified, the faculty senate (including director of core curriculum and faculty senate executive committee), and the faculty assembly. Such changes will be forwarded to the provost/vice chancellor of academic affairs for implementation.

Examples of changes falling into the respective categories are:

- Notification and access
  - Changes in policies affecting vetting procedures, record keeping, and assessment procedures within the respective units
  - Changes in courses approved for the TCU Core Curriculum (course title, number, section, instructor, course syllabi, and outcomes)
- Approval through the Faculty Senate Executive Committee
  - Changes in format, semantics, or punctuation that serve only to clarify the intent of the TCU Core Curriculum Competencies, learning outcomes, and student action steps
  - Addition of student action steps that serve to represent changing pedagogical practice in the respective fields
- Approval through the faculty assembly
  - Credit hour requirements in any portion of the TCU Core Curriculum
  - Categories as articulated in the TC Core Curriculum grid
  - Policies governing the number of areas for which any single course may be vetted or applied to the TCU Core Curriculum portion of a degree plan
  - Policies governing the number of courses carrying the same prefix (MUSI, ECON, and so on) that may be applied to any of the three main sections of the TCU Core Curriculum
  - Substantive changes to the official TCU Core Curriculum competencies, learning outcomes, and student action steps

Conclusion

Here is a summary of The Heroic Mind, a concept articulated by the eighteenth-century Italian philosopher Giambattista Vico:

> The Heroic Mind was one that leaped beyond its capacity and its preparation. The Heroic Mind exhibited a dynamic, on-going process of holistic, integrated thought and imaginative fluency. This process dialogically unified the cognitive, or critical, analytical, and conceptual, with the creative, or making capacities of the human mind. As the ultimate, but ever-eluding goal of humanistic education, the Heroic Mind used knowledge in the quest for Wisdom, Sapienta, which Vico defines as a knowledge of the whole and how the parts participate in that whole. The Heroic Mind in its Wisdom dedicates its knowledge of the whole to the service of the human community in order to articulate

and promote the sensus communis, the sense of shared, communal human experience [Fiore, 1998].

At TCU our "sensus communis" is achieved through realization of our common purpose. Each one of us is here to learn and to aid others in this endeavor. The opportunity for continued cooperation between the various stakeholders in the TCU community was especially exciting. Although the faculty through the faculty senate designed the new curriculum, implementation of the TCU Core Curriculum required the help and support of the entire TCU community, and the success of the TCU Core Curriculum will continue to require such help and support.

Curricular reform at TCU was extraordinarily rewarding, on several levels. TCU faculty from across disciplines and colleges engaged in a level of dialogue that was unprecedented on our campus. Additionally, staff in the academic and student affairs divisions were deeply involved in the process, particularly during the implementation phase. As a result, TCU now has an innovative undergraduate core curriculum that is expressed in outcome statements of student learning congruent with our institutional mission and priorities.

The process of creating the TCU Core Curriculum has reminded all of us of our commitment to the most central mission of any educational institution, the quest for wisdom, Vico's sapienta. May we impart, through the study of the essential competencies; human experiences and endeavors; and heritage, mission, vision, and values, an understanding of the past, a sense of the present, and a foundation for the greater accomplishments yet to come.

References

Allen, M. J. (2006). *Assessing general education programs*. Bolton, MA: Anker.
American Association of Colleges and Universities. (2009, May). *Trends and emerging practices in general education*. Retrieved September 24, 2009, from http://www.aacu .org/membership/documents/2009MemberSurvey_Part2.pdf.
Bok, D. (2006). Our underachieving colleges. Princeton, NJ: Princeton University Press.
Fiore, S. R. (1998). *Giambattista Vico and the pedagogy of "heroic mind" in the liberal arts*. University of South Florida, paper presented at the Twentieth World Congress of Philosophy, Boston, August 10–15. Retrieved September 24, 2009, from http://web.bu .edu/wcp/Papers/Educ/EducFior.htm.
Kuh, G. D. (2008). *High-impact educational practices: What they are, who has access to them, and why they matter*. Washington, DC: American Association of Colleges and Universities.
Texas Christian University (2009). *Faculty and Staff Handbook*. Fort Worth, TX: Texas Christian University. Retrieved from http://www.tcu.edu/files/BlackWhiteHandbook .pdf on January 7, 2010.
Washington Center (n.d.). *What are learning communities?* Olympia, Washington: The Evergreen State College. Retrieved on August 5, 2009, from http://www.evergreen .edu/washcenter/lcFaq.htm#21.

Wehlburg, C. M., & McNertney, E. M. (2009). Faculty learning communities as an assessment technique for measuring general education outcomes. In T. M. Banta, E. A. Jones, & K. E. Black (Eds.), *Designing effective assessment: Principles and profiles of good practice*. San Francisco: Jossey-Bass.

EDWARD M. MCNERTNEY *is the director of the TCU Core Curriculum and chair of TCU Department of Economics. He was an active campus leader in the effort to revise the undergraduate core curriculum serving first as a member of the Core Curriculum Committee, an ad hoc University committee constituted by the provost and tasked with the design of the TCU Core Curriculum, and, later, as chair of the Core Implementation Committee, a Faculty Senate subcommittee charged with providing oversight for implementation of the TCU Core Curriculum. Dr. McNertney also serves as the editor of the Southwestern Economic Review. He earned his Ph.D. in economics from the University of Massachusetts Amherst.*

BLAISE FERRANDINO *is an associate professor and division chair of Music Theory and Composition at Texas Christian University where he has been since 1990. From 2000–2002 he served as Interim Director of the School of Music. In addition to his work in music theory, Dr. Ferrandino is a composer and double bassist. He has served on the Core Curriculum Committee, the Heritage, Mission, Vision, and Values Committee, and the Core Implementation Committee. Dr. Ferrandino served as the chair of the TCU Faculty Senate during the 2004–2005 academic year.*

7

A college education has never been so necessary, or so expensive. It is incumbent upon us, the educators, to do it the best we can. The products of our work are not the buildings on our campuses but our students who go out into this complicated and exciting world to serve as its leaders, its citizens, and its workers. The Bates College general education curriculum is used in this chapter to articulate the importance of several integrative goals and processes that make up our new general education curriculum.

Creating an Integrative General Education: The Bates Experience

Jill Reich, Judy Head

If nothing else, the events of recent times have convinced us that we live in an era of unprecedented opportunity and immense challenge. As educators, we know that it will take breadth and depth of knowledge, flexibly positioned, if our students are to understand and make the most of the similarities and differences of intellectual approaches. Further, to be successful in this way of thinking is critical if our society is to make progress with such issues as climate change, political instability, and economic uncertainty. So, we must ask ourselves how to create in our students the courage and intellect to think in bold new ways, find the sustenance to persist in a miasma of often contradictory facts, and tolerate the ambiguity this produces. How do we help them find links across ideas we once thought were separate and develop solutions to questions we assumed had none? To aspire to these ideals and goals is no small matter. It requires all of our efforts and resources coordinated and strategically synchronized into a learning environment that is an integrated whole.

The general education program of the undergraduate curriculum offers an important opportunity to do this because it plays a major role in shaping student learning, values, and the intellectual environment. As that part of the curriculum that all students must meet, its visibility and positioning makes it a significant trademark of the institution. The type of learning, its content, and even the decision of whether or not there are requirements all serve to establish in a very public way the kind of learning each institution

NEW DIRECTIONS FOR TEACHING AND LEARNING, no. 121, Spring 2010 © Wiley Periodicals, Inc.
Published online in Wiley InterScience (www.interscience.wiley.com) • DOI: 10.1002/tl.389

seeks to achieve for its students. Current thinking about the learning process during the traditional undergraduate years calls on us to create a landscape for learning that supports and does not discourage the permeability of disciplinary boundaries, and to recognize that the rapidly increasing diversity of our students and their learning styles underscores the complex, multi-dimensional nature of the task. Thus the general education curriculum too must encompass these characteristics.

The General Education Curriculum at Bates College

To respond to a changing world, the Bates College faculty recently adopted a general education program that is integrative and responds to the developmental makeup of the population we serve, undergraduates generally between the ages of seventeen and twenty-two—years of significant growth and development. To develop breadth and depth of learning in the discipline and to garner an understanding of the complexity of this kind of knowledge, students complete a "major plus two." The "plus two" are general education concentrations, which students and faculty fondly nicknamed GECs. Each GEC is a faculty-designed collection of at least sixteen courses or a combination of courses and co-curricular units focusing on a theme or a discipline. With their advisors' assistance, students must choose from this list four courses to constitute their GEC. The GECs introduce and then build on perspectives that span the liberal arts and sciences. At its best, the GEC weaves together the humanities, social sciences, sciences, interdisciplinary studies, and co-curricular units. By linking together forms of knowledge, methodologies, styles of teaching, and ways of communicating from a variety of courses across disciplines and co-curricular opportunities, we seek to offer students an appreciation of the connectedness as well as the complexity of knowledge.

Essential companions to knowledge are abilities to think critically, analyze, read closely, investigate well, and communicate persuasively and correctly. To foster these abilities, the general education program requires that students complete three writing courses, one in the first year (W1), one in the sophomore or junior year (W2), and a third (W3), which is usually a senior thesis or capstone, in the senior year. A requirement of three separate courses in quantitative literacy (Q), laboratory experience (L), and scientific reasoning (S) ensures that students have formal instruction at the college level in these areas so that they may acquire the information and understanding necessary to approach our world with knowledge and a discerning eye.

Designing a New General Education Curriculum. How did Bates design this new curriculum, and what motivated us to do it in this way? The new general education program is the first reform of general education at the college since 1979, which is more than thirty years without a change. An attempt at reform in the nineties was unsuccessful, because the process was largely top-down and thereby lacking sufficient faculty understanding and input. We knew, consequently, that we needed to proceed thoughtfully—and we needed to be successful. As we began the discussion, we recognized that a new curriculum should build on the established traditions and values of the institution, and in so doing align the institution's history to its current interests and future aspirations.

We began in summer 2003 by sending a team of faculty and an associate dean to the Asheville Institute on General Education at the University of North Carolina, to learn from others about processes and programs so that we could inform faculty of best practices across the country. There followed in the next year important conversations among faculty and students about the goals of a Bates education. Though the yearlong discussions did not erase the failure of the past effort from all minds, it combined knowledge of best practices in general education with conversations about Bates traditions and values, which generated interest among faculty members and resulted in a discussion and consensus about educational objectives for our students and ways to achieve them.

An approach we learned from the 2003 Asheville Institute meeting gave us an important strategy. It used a two-committee structure: first, a four-person design team, and second, an elected coordinating committee of ten faculty members and the dean. This structure allowed us to have a small, focused group looking deeply at how to organize and design the curriculum, at the same time that we had a larger group engaging faculty in ongoing discussions about the ideas and options being explored. This kind of ongoing communication with faculty was essential in building momentum and support. Discussions of the emerging design continued through open meetings, meetings with departments and programs, faculty meetings, individual conversations, celebrations of steps accomplished, e-mails, minutes, and postings on Web pages. At key decision points, we included all faculty by asking them to vote on their readiness to continue moving toward legislating a final design curriculum. The new general legislation curriculum was adopted in March 2006 by approval of more than 80 percent of the faculty and was scheduled to begin in fall 2007. The one-year delay was necessary to develop, tweak, and align courses, to work out details of curriculum management, and to build software to meet the new requirements.

Challenges of the New Curriculum: Implementation. Educators at liberal arts colleges have a unique opportunity to take advantage of the breadth, depth, and intimacy of an intellectual setting that looks across disciplines and weaves interdisciplinarity into their programs. At the same time, we cannot build departments, faculty, and curricula around every good idea. Rather, we must develop structures that give focus and intellectual integrity to our curricula while retaining flexibility so as to be responsive to new ideas and ways of thinking. Instead of generating a new writing program, for example, we drew on our first-year seminar program and senior theses, both of which have existed at the college for decades. Courses in quantitative literacy, laboratory experience, and scientific reasoning have a

NEW DIRECTIONS FOR TEACHING AND LEARNING • DOI: 10.1002/tl

long and strong history at Bates. The new curriculum has stimulated our scientists and mathematicians to develop new ways to connect them. Our GECs build on courses and co-curricular elements already part of the curricula of our departments and programs, but they encourage faculty to think about strengthening existing connections and building new ones.

Consequently our new general education curriculum builds on existing programs by connecting and augmenting them in new ways, which in turn calls for new oversight. Faculty must create GECs and designate courses as writing-attentive or as having appropriate quantitative or scientific content. Not wanting to add still more committees to our governance, our first-year seminar and writing committee oversee writing while our educational policy committee administers general education and its implementation as a whole.

As expected, implementation is an ongoing process. As our new general education curriculum matures, we continuously construct and study assessment processes, address pedagogical needs and resources, enhance support for students and faculty development, and study and respond to other needs and issues so that we are meeting the explicit goals set forth for the general education curriculum.

Opportunities of the New Curriculum: Integrated Learning. An essential challenge facing educators is creating curricula, co-curricula, and educational systems that nurture and embrace the limitless nature of ideas and knowledge within the very real limitations of our organizations. The curriculum must be able to easily integrate the ideas, intellectual searching, and problem solving that the questions of today and challenges of tomorrow demand. No longer is there an established canon, theory, or paradigm whose mastery defines the educated person.

Preparing our students to think innovatively and beyond conventional boundaries is a critical aspect of what we do. Indeed, some of the most exciting learning and investigations take place in the areas between disciplines and established academic areas.

The small liberal arts college is a rich setting for capitalizing on opportunities to cross disciplinary and intellectual boundaries because faculty do so all of the time. Small departments necessarily encourage faculty to reach across intellectual boundaries to find new homes and colleagues for their ideas and research. When students follow, they learn more broadly and become more astute thinkers. They grasp the complexity of an area of inquiry if offered more than one perspective. At the same time, cross-disciplinary learning introduces students to multiple modes of analysis, ways of thinking, and approaches to learning.

By showing our students multiple ways of perceiving an issue or area of learning and a variety of methods of analysis and investigation, we mold learners who are nimble in intellect, broad in communication, and adaptable in applying their ideas. They have a range of knowledge and develop an intellectual energy that propels their learning. Faculty savor those occasions when a student tells them that, because of a reading, discussion, film, or experience in a class in another discipline or an experience outside the college, he or she sees a historical event, a piece of literature, or an environmental issue in a new way. It is these "aha" moments, these instances when students make an intellectual connection or leap, that we value most as educators and seek to capture in our assessment as evidence of our achievement.

General Education Concentrations: Connected Learning

General education concentrations are of particular interest to our efforts to promote integrative learning. We believe that GECs foster moments of revelation. We designed GECs to furnish a structure that offers students broad knowledge to help them navigate methodologies, theories, modes of learning, and communication. GECs focused on themes or topics call on students to cross traditional academic boundaries.

In the concentration "The City in History: Urbanism and Constructed Spaces," for example, students are required to weave together knowledge about cities and urban life as viewed through the lens of a variety of disciplines. They must read and learn to think, research, and write in ways appropriate to a number of disciplines. In the process, the stimulation of investigating and looking at a subject from multiple points of view with faculty and peers who have like interests invigorates and motivates them to make new and productive connections.

In "The City in History" a variety of routes are open to students; they choose those of greatest interest. The GEC requires four courses, no more than two of which may be from any one department or program. Students may look in depth at the central European cities of Berlin and Vienna through the eyes of literary studies, or they may study a variety of cities in Latin America through a historical lens. Italian and Dutch cities come to life through art and the lives of artists who painted their landscapes and their inhabitants. Another course in the GEC uses the tools of economics to look at urbanization through studies of industry, development, and settlement.

In "Place, Word, Sound: New Orleans," the hub of the Mississippi delta comes alive through its culture and location. Students may choose a research project, internship, fieldwork, performance experience, volunteer work, or community work-study as an optional co-curricular element of the GEC. In both GECs students are exposed to different ways of looking at urban life and development. They read, look at, and listen to an array of materials. They may be part of a hands-on experience in community-based learning in our small city or in a larger one. In every case, they are asked to think, research, and communicate like scholars in several disciplines, whether it be history, art, economics, or literature. They must look at a common theme using a variety of methodologies.

Another example that captures the spirit and direction of what we seek to achieve in our multidisciplinary GECs is "Color: Sight and Perception."

In it young learners wander among disciplines as diverse as art, biology, philosophy, physics, psychology, and film to understand how scholars approach color using multiple perspectives. In courses such as "Imaging Details: The Quest for Resolution or Physics in Everyday Life," they learn how physicists understand, describe, and measure color. Students learn how color fits into photography in the course "The Digital Image" or into painting in "Color and Design." They also study the impact of skin color on society in the course "White Redemption: Cinema and the Co-optation of African American History." Students can also ask how might biologists explain our perception of color? They can discover this in in the course on "Sensory Biology."

As students absorb knowledge and read about, discuss, and consider color from the point of view of scholars from various fields, they come to know color as a complex idea, measured in a variety of ways, answering a number of questions, and applied to a range of interests.

By fostering thinking and learning across disciplines, our four-component GECs are fundamental building blocks of our general education curriculum. Linking disciplines by concentrating on themes gives students the opportunity to make connections among ways of thinking; build and appreciate the skills of critical thinking, problem solving, analysis, and communication in several disciplines; and so come to know the strengths and complexity of knowledge.

Advances in our New Curriculum: Co-curricular Learning

Not only do the GECs impart a structure to extend across disciplinary boundaries, but they also encourage the curriculum to be flexible enough to integrate the variety of pedagogies needed to realize each student's potential for learning. The days of a traditional classroom as the only place for learning are gone. In fact, the classroom might better be considered a scaffold for learning, the structure that supports the variety of pedagogies and venues ranging from civic engagement to other co-curricular opportunities that make up our learning environments.

Bringing experiences outside the classroom into general education programs fosters integrative education by introducing our students to the multifaceted nature of knowledge and validating their learning in all of its forms and sources. Learning beyond the classroom also offers opportunities for students of various talents and interests to acquire and apply knowledge in diverse ways. It promotes vital awareness of the world beyond our institutions and understanding of how higher education fits comfortably there.

Many of our four-part GECs include co-curricular units, which serve as components of the GEC, as part of its courses within the GEC, or as a supplement to the GEC. A few examples will bring home the importance of the co-curricular elements as components of student learning within the concentrations. The GEC "Public Health," for example, requires a community-based learning component. Students may choose from summer work in a clinic or nutritional center in our community. Alternately, students may enroll in courses such as Medicine and Culture in the department of anthropology or Health Psychology in the department of psychology, both of which include a strong community-based learning component. Teaching students about public health issues from perspectives that range from private practice to public policy and from the sociology of race, class, and gender in health care to cultural constructions of health and sickness is best accomplished by testing theories and data against real-world experiences.

We are fortunate to have the resources of the Harward Center for Community Partnerships, which partners with more than two dozen community organizations, including clinics and hospitals, to oversee and guide this work. The Carnegie Foundation for the Advancement of Teaching awarded Bates and the Harward Center its Community Engagement Classification, created to recognize colleges and universities that have institutionalized community engagement in their endeavors.

Other GECs also incorporate learning on campus, but in settings outside conventional classrooms. The Collaborative Project pursues its objective of generating "action, original work, and/or live performance" by requiring students to complete a co-curricular component. Possibilities include two semesters in musical ensemble, whether orchestra or choice, fiddle band, gamelan, steel pans, or jazz band; doing a planetarium production; or creating a performance in dance, music, or theater. A number of GECs linked to the sciences include components that range from work with a professor on a research project during summer months to an NSF Research Experiences for Undergraduates (REU) internship.

Co-curricular elements may also be part of writing components of our general education curriculum, from first-level writing courses (W1) to senior theses that must exhibit proficiency in the major and senior-level writing competence (W3). "Literature Through Cataclysm," a first-year seminar that looks at extraordinary change in several global societies, includes a service-learning project with members of our local Somali community who have survived cataclysm. Seniors in psychology and sociology may choose a senior thesis or senior-level writing (W3) component that combines community-based learning and academic research and writing. As part of their community-based thesis experience, students meet regularly to discuss ethics and cultural contexts of their work in the community. These meetings supply the theory and data that ground their learning in the disciplines and offer opportunities for reflection that integrates their experiences with their growing knowledge. We find that the GECs of our new curriculum are a particularly rich format for integrating co-curricular learning into the college experience.

Growing with Our Students: Developmental Learning

As we considered and planned a general education program that would prepare our students to navigate and contribute to the modern world, we thought about the period of time for which we have our students with us. Given this period in their lives, how do we best help them evolve from high school graduates into college learners who possess significant knowledge; who think deeply, broadly, and critically; and who communicate well? Because our traditional undergraduate students are in the throes of significant growth and development, we aimed to design a learning environment that integrates with their development and stretches their intellectual growth. Their skills and achievements are not static during the college years. Consequently, faculty must be aware of their developmental stages and adopt appropriate strategies to fit them.

Generally, institutions of higher education structure courses developmentally, with students acquiring skills and knowledge in lower-level courses before they can succeed in advanced ones. As students progress, we ask that they engage in ever more sophisticated thinking and deploy increasingly complex methodologies. Yet we rarely do this within our general education curriculum, where courses most often are considered entry-level and designed to "be completed" so that students may move on to their "real" interests. Believing strongly in our general education curriculum, we believed that a crucial objective in the design of the program was to include the academic and intellectual development that occurs between the first and fourth year. Our three-tiered writing requirement is a clear example of our approach.

Writing at Bates is not a requirement our students "get out of the way" by completing a course or two during their first year. We believe that writing generates thinking; to write well, students must think well. Because first-year students neither think nor write at the advanced level of students in the upper classes, our faculty adopted a program that places greater demands on them as they mature and develop as scholars. Students begin with a writing-attentive course in their first year and revisit writing at least once in their middle years and again as seniors.

Though first-year seminars are not required, 98–99 percent of our incoming students complete their first-year writing requirement in these courses. Rather than focusing only on content, the first-year seminars (with fifteen or fewer students) emphasize writing, class participation, analytical thinking, and research. Faculty teaching first-year seminars meet regularly throughout the year to talk about pedagogy, especially around writing, advising their students, and challenges they and their students may be facing.

The second-level writing course, or W2, required during the sophomore or junior year, builds on the skills learned and thinking developed in the W1. Though courses vary, many W2s call on students to research, write, cite, and think more deeply in the discipline. Many W2s also pay close attention to the methodology of a discipline or course of study. W3 courses, taken at the senior level, are usually theses or in some cases capstone experiences that involve civic engagement. These courses require higher-level knowledge in the major and the ability to think and communicate well. By adopting a writing requirement that continues throughout students' educational careers, faculty ensured that writing, and the thinking, reflection, and communication skills that the word *writing* signifies, expands with our students, challenging them as they mature as thinkers and learners.

Our general education concentrations also capture the developmental nature of our recent plan. Again, GECs grow with our students rather than being components that students complete in their first and second years. GECs offer courses across a range of levels and difficulties so that students address the topic at a more complex level as their skills and learning advance. In "The Human Body" students may look at the human body through biological and physiological eyes in courses such as "Extreme Physiology" and "Sensory Biology," which lead to "Comparative Anatomy of Cordates," "Animal Physiology," and "Physiological Psychology." A lower-level women and gender studies course, "Technologies of the Body," leads students to "Gender and Technology," a higher-level course. Students might begin with a first-year seminar, "Corporate Culture: Body and Health in America," and move on to an anthropology course, "Medicine and Culture," which is also part of the concentration on "Public Health." In ways that mirror but expand on curricula within academic disciplines, courses in writing and within GECs grow with our students. As students develop greater skill in critical thinking, they learn more advanced ways to use evidence and analysis; as they develop greater facility in communicating their thoughts and insights, they move on to writing courses and components in GECs that challenge and stretch them by asking that they use their learning in more complex situations and with more complicated problems. Designing a general education curriculum that demands increasing levels of learning, skill, and effort meshes well with and further develops the growth and maturity of our students during their time at Bates.

Conclusion

A college education has never been so necessary, or so expensive. It is incumbent upon us, the educators, to do the best we can to prepare our students for their future. The products of our work are not the buildings on our campuses but our students who go out into this complicated and exciting world to serve as its leaders, its citizens, and its workers. What they will accomplish depends in part on the tools, the ways of thinking, and the perspectives on learning and knowledge that they gain from their time with us. Will they be able to learn in the new ways demanded by the questions of today and tomorrow? Will they adapt to new methods of working, and be nimble and confident in their problem-solving abilities? Will they be able to communicate well their ideas and potential contributions? These are the hurdles we face as we develop goals for our curricula and build our learning environments. At Bates we are excited by these challenging questions that directed the design of our new general education curriculum.

JILL REICH is vice president of Academic Affairs and dean of the Faculty at Bates College. She received her B.A. from Regis College and her Ph.D. in Experimental Psychology from Dartmouth. She has consulted with the American Academy of Pediatrics, the Illinois Legislature, and WHS&A architects and planners. In addition, Dr. Reich served as executive director of Education for the American Psychological Association and as dean of the Faculty at Trinity College in Connecticut.

JUDY HEAD is an associate dean of the Faculty and lecturer in history at Bates College whose work has resulted in development of programs for assessing first year writing, student learning in the major, senior theses, and writing at the senior level. She continues to work with faculty and staff to clearly articulate and fulfill goals related to the new General Education curriculum. She received her B.A. and M.A. from the University of Oklahoma and her Ph.D. from the University of Texas at Austin.

NEW DIRECTIONS FOR TEACHING AND LEARNING • DOI: 10.1002/tl

8

Using experiences from three institutions, the authors describe a three-stage process for designing an integrated general education program that takes into account institutional differences. The three stages are (1) establishing initial discussions that lead to alignment of key university SLOs with key general education SLOs, (2) training and workshopping with faculty groups and administrators whose first task usually is to work with the key general education outcomes and select the appropriate measures for them, and (3) training and workshopping with faculty groups who teach the junior and senior courses that most majors take (the required courses, or courses such as senior capstones) to develop and establish course-embedded assessment in the assessment plans of the degree programs.

Building an Integrated Student Learning Outcomes Assessment for General Education: Three Case Studies

Jo K. Galle, Jeffery Galle

Lynn Priddy of the Higher Learning Commission, in a plenary address at the 2009 annual conference of the Association of General and Liberal Studies, urged institutions to begin with the mission and vision of their institution in aligning assessment efforts across the institution. Although such a laudable idea is perhaps the most logical and fundamental approach, many institutions actually back into the assessment process before the question or issue of integration of outcomes is ever brought up. Whatever the initial impetus for entering the process, gradual development of assessment efforts suggests that success with integrating learning outcomes will evolve through a set of stages. This chapter outlines the paths of three institutions toward integration of learning outcomes through three generally defined stages: (1) the impetus toward designing outcomes assessment that emerges from a number of possible sources with accompanying workshops and meetings for faculty and administrators, (2) focused development of some of the phases of outcomes assessment and measures in one or more areas at

New Directions for Teaching and Learning, no. 121, Spring 2010 © Wiley Periodicals, Inc.
Published online in Wiley InterScience (www.interscience.wiley.com) • DOI: 10.1002/tl.390

the same time, and (3) discussions having an impact on completion of the alignment process.

Each of the three institutions outlined in this chapter—the University of Louisiana at Monroe, Oxford College of Emory University, and Southern Polytechnic State University—began the assessment process for its own reasons and in a distinct institutional context. Yet, as different as they are, what they share is the set of roughly defined stages. In addition, the process is still ongoing at all three institutions. What we did find, however, is the usefulness of conceptualizing these efforts as having these three distinct phases. That is, although the outcomes and alignment are what institutions may inevitably come to value, they arrive at this juncture through these three stages. Identifying differences within this commonality may enable other institutions to locate reasons where they are at in the process, and perhaps why their efforts toward integrated outcomes assessment are faltering or are not moving forward as effectively as they might.

The possibilities deserve some mention. Some institutions begin with program-level student learning outcomes (SLOs) and establish them, along with appropriate measures, before proceeding "backward" to general education or "upward" to university learning outcomes. Frequently, however, institutions use general education reform as the primary modus to create program-level SLOs, and perhaps these will link up with strategic planning and a learning outcomes discussion at the university level. In most cases, the idea of developing assessment programs arrives at the doorstep of institutions with a lot already going on. Therefore, in reality, assessment develops in more than one way. Some institutions implement general education assessment programs first, followed by development of program outcomes and then university outcomes, while other institutions design the various types of outcomes assessment in a totally different order. If an institution prefers to have the three types—university, general education, and program outcomes—then perhaps the ideal pattern would be to form university student learning outcomes first, followed by general education and then program outcomes. If an institution prefers to have its general education outcomes serve as university outcomes and be aligned with program outcomes, then perhaps the ideal would be to have the faculty and administrators at that institution first review its general education outcomes and then review and align its program outcomes with them. In reality, working with any of the three primary ingredients of an integrated outcomes assessment program involves complex institutional processes that are already under way.

Beginning the Process

For the University of Louisiana at Monroe, the shift to a learning outcomes model roughly began with creation of a new core curriculum. Not linked at first to an alignment of outcomes, the overhaul of the old core curriculum involved creating a University Core Curriculum Committee (UCC). This entity placed a series of meetings on the university calendar. What emerged from that committee and its overlap of several members with the UCC was a set of six general education SLOs:

1. A student will be able to explore the interrelationship of knowledge in our increasingly global society.
2. A student will be able to examine the people, values, and societies of both Eastern and Western civilizations.
3. A student will develop the global perspective necessary for living and working in a world economy.
4. A student will be able to adapt to an ever-changing international environment.
5. A student will develop writing and/or communication skills.
6. A student will develop research/creative skills [http://www.ulm.edu/assessment/documents/oae_handbook.pdf].

After a year of discussion, the assessment plan for measuring these six general education SLOs was developed. This process involved selecting appropriate measure(s), protocols for reporting of assessment data, and an opportunity to describe a use-of-results response in courses that involve the outcome.

This list of six general education SLOs and the process described here may suggest streamlined simplicity, but what actually occurred on this campus was much more involved. In addition to the regularly scheduled meetings of the UCC, a series of universitywide forums occurred over the course of the academic year, a university Web site including FAQs and question-and-answer sessions with the committee was developed, and the UCC regularly hosted faculty guest presenters who spoke about their perspectives on general education reform. For many faculty members, this process became the basis for a discussion of learning goals that carried over into individual departments offering the general education courses. As a result, the first phase of outcomes discussion on the University of Louisiana at Monroe campus involved these multiple UCC meetings and curricular discussion in the College of Arts and Sciences, which houses the general education courses.

For Oxford College of Emory University, "signature outcomes" discussion began as the central topic for the 2008 fall faculty retreat. A professional facilitator was hired to guide the various meetings, breakout sessions, and the general direction of the full day. The retreat began with a morning meeting at which various answers were posed to the general questions, "What is an Oxford College of Emory University education?" and "What has an Oxford College graduate come to possess in terms of knowledge, skills, and attitude?" Breakout sessions, multiple group meetings, and two meals followed, with the daylong process culminating in refinement of seven "values" or "outcomes" of an Oxford College education:

New Directions for Teaching and Learning • DOI: 10.1002/tl

1. *Ars Liberalis.* The liberal arts commitment to and awareness of integrative learning
2. *Mind/body/spirit/nature.* Commitment to holistic well-being
3. *Challenge seeking.* Commitment to ask and face the most complex and difficult questions and issues
4. *Critical thinking.* Systematic cultivation of the examination of premises, arguments, values, and implications of thought; thinking on thinking
5. *Engaged citizenship from local to global.* Commitment to leadership
6. *Communication, both written and oral.* Commitment to skilled communication
7. *Passionate learning.* Commitment to lifelong, in-depth, devoted learning

At the conclusion of the faculty retreat, these signature outcomes of an Oxford College education were turned over to the college's Liberal Arts Intensive Committee for further work, consideration, combination, and refinement.

The initial impetus for Southern Polytechnic State University (SPSU) was the university's need to prepare for a self-study review by the regional accreditor, the Southern Association for Colleges and Schools (SACS) Commission on Colleges. Discussions began across campus about the need to enhance student learning outcomes assessment. In particular, a key part of the initial discussion involved revision of the general education outcomes. Consequently, over the course of several months ten university core curriculum outcomes were adopted.

The general education outcomes at SPSU were the result of numerous discussions that began in the College of Arts and Sciences, and the dean and the chairs met regularly to refine them. Then the discussions of this small group of members expanded as the chairs began deliberating the outcomes at their regular departmental faculty meetings. Eventually, it went to the faculty senate, and the senate voted to accept the ten outcomes. Southern Polytechnic has published these outcomes on its Web site (http://www.spsu.edu/irpa/CoreCurriculumLearningOutcomes.htm):

> All graduates of Southern Polytechnic State University will be able to:
> Demonstrate an ability to analyze and interpret oral and written arguments and materials
> Demonstrate an ability to write and communicate effectively in various modes and media
> Express and manipulate mathematical information, concepts, and thoughts in verbal, numeric, graphical, and symbolic form while solving a variety of problems
> Use statistics and/or formulae to understand quantitative data
> Demonstrate an ability to solve multiple-step problems through different (inductive, deductive, and symbolic) modes of reasoning
> Describe the historical evolution and contemporary impact of political, economic, and social relationships within and between nations

Demonstrate an ability to describe, and explain the significance of, common-
alities and differences among human cultures
Understand and apply basic scientific principles, theories, and laws
Critically analyze the role in and impact of science and technology on society
Demonstrate an ability to make informed aesthetic judgments about the arts,
such as visual, performing, and literary

Another strategic move by the administration to enhance assessment of
student learning at SPSU involved conducting a national search for a
new institutional effectiveness (IE) and assessment expert from outside the
university, which was followed by initiation of meetings between the new
director of IE and the Academic Affairs office. Consequently, outcomes
assessment at SPSU began with the higher administration, and this discussion with the new director of Institutional Effectiveness and planning cul-
minated in the creation of templates both for general education outcomes
and program outcomes. This background work by the director and the vice
president of academic affairs needed to be completed and set in place before
universitywide conversations could be most profitably held. The results of
this approach meant that the administrators and the director on the leadership team at the university were the constituencies most influencing production of templates and processes that were to be used in broader discussions
at the departmental and college levels. Then the VPAA and the director presented the templates and information to the deans and the chairs at the vice
president of academic affairs meetings.

Therefore, at SPSU outcomes assessment began with general education
discussions and expanded to creation of templates for measuring the general education outcomes that were adopted as well as to establishment of
templates for measuring program outcomes.

Sustained Development

In this phase, sustained development is the hallmark. What began initially
as a series of discussions about key outcomes becomes a more concerted
effort to limit and refine broad outcomes, develop plans for assessing them,
and come up with specific measures. In this second stage, a great deal of
work is devoted to extending the initial conversations and to focusing the
subsequent dialogue on more concrete and specific next steps in whatever
particular context the institution works first. If the area is general education, dialogue of faculty committees will focus on which courses best cor-
relate with and concretely measure progress toward the general education
SLOs adopted by the institution. Also, the most significant and revelatory
measures from within the key courses will be selected. If the focus is on
learning outcomes of individual curricula, then the dialogue will involve
training faculty and administrators in development of course-embedded
assignments.

At the University of Louisiana at Monroe, the IE director and staff eventually conducted four types of training sessions for four sets of faculty and administrators.

First, the IE director met with the deans, associate deans, and the vice president of academic affairs to conduct the same type of extensive training offered by an outside expert. Essentially, these discussions ranged from program outcomes to general education and university outcomes. Some groups, notably the College of Arts and Sciences, carried the bulk of the general education courses, so this affected discussion directly, while other colleges and departments naturally gravitated toward their program outcomes. At the same time, the arts and sciences departments possessed upper-level programs that would require program outcomes as well. Eventually, after these sets of meetings were conducted, the IE director met with each dean and his or her chairs of the departments in each college to offer them the same kind of work with developing embedded assignments and assessment of outcomes practice. The third set of meetings involved the IE director's participation with individual departments and talking with the chair and the faculty in the approximately forty departments across campus to help the faculty and the chair in each discipline develop the outcomes and measures to be used in the templates. The fourth set of discussions involved the IE director presenting workshops on assessment at the faculty development center. All of the faculty and administrators from any discipline could attend these sessions, bring their own materials from their own departments, and ask questions. The director of IE used PowerPoint slides, distributed handouts, and brought samples of assessment templates and results from other universities to help the attendees learn more about how to choose measures and courses to assess their outcomes and how to use the results once the data had been collected.

By the completion of this phase, a password-protected Web site had been developed where the data for program outcomes and general education assessment data were to be stored. Also, to assess program outcomes the chairs, faculty, and administration agreed to use a four-column template and a Use of Assessment Results report form. The program outcomes, at least two courses in which the outcomes were taught, and key measures from these courses and targeted performance indicators were selected by the chairs and faculty at the beginning of the academic year. Then, at the end of the academic year, student scores were entered into the fourth column of the template, and the chair and the faculty completed the Use of Assessment Results report.

To assess general education, the chairs of those departments that housed general education filled out a template. The chair aligned the appropriate outcomes of the courses in the discipline with the corresponding university general education outcome; chose key measures and performance indicators for the course outcomes; and then, at the end of the data collection period, entered the results of the measures and completed a use report.

NEW DIRECTIONS FOR TEACHING AND LEARNING • DOI: 10.1002/tl

At Emory's Oxford College, the second phase began with training a newly hired institutional research (IR) person and a newly hired faculty development person who undertook extensive assessment training in several areas: work with indirect measures such as surveys (NSSE, Wabash Study, for example) as well as with direct measures of student work through embedded assignments. Then, to move work with the results of the initial discussions forward, the outcomes of the faculty retreat were submitted to a campus committee, the Liberal Arts Intensive Committee (LAI). Multiple presentations were given at successive LAI meetings, with a representative of each fall breakout session explaining the reasoning of the group that led to conceptualization of the eight outcomes of an Oxford College education. The LAI deliberated for some time and ultimately considered various combinations of outcomes that could be clustered together before eventually settling on a shorter list of three outcomes that are hallmarks of the Oxford education: (1) written and oral communication skills, (2) leadership, and (3) critical thinking.

At Southern Polytechnic State University, the director of institutional effectiveness had developed the plans for assessment of both general education and program outcomes with the vice president of academic affairs; then the vice president and the director presented the plans to the deans and chairs. After this initial phase, the second step was for the director to go to the chairs of the individual departments and meet with them. Subsequently, the chairs met with their faculty and discussed assessment plans. The chairs then filled out the templates, and at the end of the data collection period they also entered scores and submitted Use of Assessment Results reports.

This method worked extremely well at SPSU. If the chairs had a question, they contacted the IE director. Sometimes the chair and the director met again to discuss a particular detail. This hands-on, individualized approach, in contrast to conducting workshops in the departments and also workshops at the faculty development center (both of which had been done at the larger University of Louisiana at Monroe), proved to be the most effective technique at this university specializing in degrees that focus on technology and the sciences.

Alignment

Alignment of upper-level course and program outcomes with university and general education goals is established through working with select faculty who teach junior and senior courses and who will undertake the same kind of course-embedded work. Faculty who teach courses required for the major or those who teach courses that a high number of majors will take can be prepared to create upper-level course links between the general education and university SLOs and SLOs within specific upper-level courses.

NEW DIRECTIONS FOR TEACHING AND LEARNING • DOI: 10.1002/tl

This phase is often conducted last, since general education assessment and program outcomes assessment are required by accrediting bodies. By this time too, usually a year or more has elapsed since the initial phase and the impetus for creating a comprehensive program of assessment have occurred. Thus, when administrators and faculty begin this phase, they are aware that they have finished the key pieces and that the piece they are still seeking is one that will help the institution but is not required.

At the University of Louisiana at Monroe, initial conversation about alignment was begun with the vice president and the IE director. It was decided that two courses of action were possible. Because the university adopted six general education outcomes, the chairs and deans of the various disciplines could choose to align appropriate program outcomes from the assessment plans of their disciplines with the outcomes. This process would require the director of IE to again conduct training sessions with the chairs, faculty, and deans to illustrate how this process could be accomplished.

In spring 2009, a series of meetings were held to develop measures for at least two of these three outcomes, with the result being the Assessment Plan for Oxford College of Emory University, 2009–2011. For Oxford College, two major events prompted further discussion about alignment and any "unfinished business" regarding outcomes. First, the Emory University fifth-year SACS review was on the horizon, and the university hosted a two-day workshop with an external assessment consultant. Then Emory College changed its general education requirements and Oxford College faced the necessity of responding to this change.

At Southern Polytechnic State University, after the process of developing general education and program outcomes assessment was completed, the vice president of academic affairs and the IE director met to discuss alignment of these two types of outcomes. The first discussion involved whether to ask the chairs and faculty of programs in the various disciplines to align with the appropriate ones of the ten general education outcomes that had been designed. Another option was to form a small committee that would choose a smaller number of about five or so of these ten with which program outcomes could be aligned, or else its members could choose some of these ten and also write some new outcomes with which program outcomes could be aligned if they felt this to be best for the institution.

However, because SPSU was also completing the draft of its Quality Enhancement Plan, which is required by SACS, the decision was made to wait until after the QEP was submitted and accepted to look at the issue again.

Conclusion

In preparing even the simplest dishes, one learns not only which ingredients to use but also their proper order, the particular manner they are to be mixed, and the length of time dedicated to each step. All work together to determine whether the result is angel food cake or an uneven mound of sad-looking dough. With integrated outcomes assessment, sequenced steps for preparation seem less rigid although the process feels more complex at the same time. Consider the three primary ingredients: general education student learning outcomes, university SLOs, and program SLOs. Align these three kinds of outcomes (in some proportion), or in some cases at some institutions two kinds, and the result will be a program of integrated learning outcomes. As those with the benefit of some experience attempting this alignment may say, the process looks deceptively simple.

These assessment processes take time, usually one to three years. As these three case studies indicate, institutions for various reasons do not always commit to completing all three phases of the process: development of general education assessment plans, development of program outcome assessment plans, and alignment of either a set of university student learning outcomes or the general education outcomes already developed with the program outcomes of various disciplines. What is compelling, however, is the distinctive way in which the efforts have been undertaken at such disparate institutions.

As we have also seen in these three case studies, the process of development varies. Aligning these sets of learning outcomes is a process often unique to an institution, rather than a logical, universal process such as that suggested by Priddy at the beginning of this chapter. In fact, in each of the three institutions covered in this chapter, the process of alignment began and ended at different points. In none of them was the process entirely complete. Yet in each case, the institution took demonstrable steps toward a learning outcomes model, and each institution can see the next steps toward alignment.

Jo K. Galle is the associate vice-president for Academic Affairs at Georgia Gwinnett College. Prior to serving in this position, she was the director of Institutional Effectiveness and Planning at Southern Polytechnic State University and the director of Assessment and Evaluation at the University of Louisiana–Monroe, respectively. Galle also has worked with the Commission on Colleges of the Southern Association as an outside evaluator. She earned her Ph.D. in English at Louisiana State University.

Jeffery Galle is the director of the Center for Academic Excellence at Oxford College of Emory University. Galle, selected for the Distinguished Teaching Scholar recognition at Emory University, organizes a number of the faculty programs of Oxford College, including the Institute for Pedagogy in the Liberal Arts. His recent pedagogical research, in addition to assessment, has focused upon blended learning, rubrics and writing courses, and the use of historical archives and life writing. Dr. Galle completed his undergraduate work and the M.A. at Louisiana Tech University, and he received the Ph.D. from Louisiana State University.

New Directions for Teaching and Learning • DOI: 10.1002/tl

9

This chapter describes a transformative approach to assessing general education programs, identifies potential obstacles to successful assessment, and outlines necessary steps for creating assessable, outcomes-based programs.

Meaningful General Education Assessment That Is Integrated and Transformative

Catherine M. Wehlburg

Assessing general education is not that different from assessing any other type of academic program, but there are some distinctions that make it even more challenging than other types of assessment. This chapter addresses methods for working with nondepartmentally based and interdisciplinary areas within general education, providing some examples of these types of assessment activities. In addition, assessing an integrated general education program is one thing; actually integrating the findings can be quite another. Methods for gathering and interpreting disparate pieces of general education assessment findings (even one that is integrated) are shared.

Assessment practices in higher education may have been receiving additional attention lately, but these practices are certainly nothing new. The argument can be made that assessment of student learning is so intertwined with teaching and learning that assessment and teaching are actually "two sides of the same coin" (Wehlburg, 2010, p. 242). Recently, however, with the focus on assessing student learning outcomes as a requirement for all regional and many specialized accreditors, the term *assessment* has been understood as a method for identifying student learning goals and outcomes, gathering data to demonstrate learning, and then using the results to make improvements so that students' learning increases.

Assessing program and disciplinary areas has been practiced widely for more than a decade. But assessing general education programs is a newer

NEW DIRECTIONS FOR TEACHING AND LEARNING, no. 121, Spring 2010   © Wiley Periodicals, Inc.
Published online in Wiley InterScience (www.interscience.wiley.com) • DOI: 10.1002/tl.391

focus. Because most majors assess content and skills, many of them with "built in" measures within required and capstone courses, progress in assessment has been relatively steady. Faculty may not enjoy the assessment process, but it is usually considered to be at least a task that must be done, if not enjoyed. On the other hand, assessing general education has been more difficult. Part of this is that the overall goals of general education tend to be less specific and more difficult to measure. Goals of critical thinking, problem solving, and communication are difficult to define in ways that are measurable. Attempting to quantify some of these higher-order thinking skills is very difficult, if not impossible. Qualitative assessment data are useful, but many faculty are not as comfortable with using qualitative data to assess general education. Further, faculty do not have as strong a feeling of ownership over general education as they do with their disciplinary home. As Marinara, Vajravelu, and Young (2004) indicate, "except in rare cases, the general education program is not really constructed as a 'program' in the same sense that majors are" (p. 1).

Unfortunately, assessment as a whole has been used as a tool for accountability and accreditation. This has been especially true for general education assessment. Integration of general education assessment has been difficult in part because the overall integration of general education goals has not been well integrated for many institutions. Without an integrated concept of which general educations goals students should reach, designing effective assessment plans cannot occur.

Shulman (2007) described assessment as using data to tell the story of an educational program. In this metaphor, assessment is the process for gathering the information to build a narrative that can be shared with others:

> The story told by an assessment is thus ultimately a function of the dimensions of measurement that determine the possible directions the narrative might take. So accountability requires that we take responsibility for the story we commit ourselves to telling. We must make public the rationale for choosing that story as opposed to alternative narratives . . . only then should we defend the adequacy of the forms of measurement and documentation we employ to warrant the narratives we offer" [p. 22].

Viewing general education assessment as a means of sharing information is necessary, but not sufficient. Assessment of a general education program must be embedded in how the faculty, the departments, and the entire institution gather meaningful information about student learning within the context of the overall mission and goals of the local institution. The faculty must give voice to the "story" of learning in higher education because it is only with participation by faculty and use of the assessment process that the true story of an integrated general education program can be fully shared.

Student learning assessment is "the systematic collection of information about student learning, using the time, knowledge, expertise, and resources available, in order to inform decisions about how to improve learning" (Walvoord, 2004, p. 2). The significant part of this definition is that assessment is done for the purpose of informing decision making about improving student learning. Assessment of student learning has become something that is done for others, rather than for its original purpose. General education assessment data can and will be used for accountability; certainly, parents, potential students, and the public deserve to know what higher education is doing in the area of general education. Accountability has an important role, but to only gather general education assessment data to show others what is occurring seems to be a large, time-consuming task that will never affect or inform decision making about what students are learning as a result of an institution's general education program.

Transformative assessment is a process that is appropriate, meaningful, sustainable, flexible, and ongoing, and that uses data for improvement (Wehlburg, 2008). Even though data that are collected can also be used to demonstrate outcomes to others, transformative assessment is focused on how to enhance student learning. Each element of transformative assessment is essential, but because of the differing missions, institutional cultures, and needs each may be implemented differently. General education assessment should be a transformative process for better integration into the overall educational ethos of the institution. However, to do this well general education assessment plans must have meaningful goals, measurable outcomes, measures that can be done in the time available, and faculty consensus for the entire process.

Creating Outcomes-Based General Education

Individual courses exist for a specific reason: they are designed to ensure that students learn and use the content about a particular subject and their associated skills. Courses also are created so that the sum of a set of courses leads into a major or a degree. With general education, however, courses are often chosen because of their prefix or departmental home rather than their content. In other words, a sociology course could be chosen to meet a social sciences requirement regardless of the type of content taught in the course. Contrast that, however, with a planned, outcomes-based general education program in which courses are chosen to be included because the content of a course aligns with a specific outcome. With this, courses are still taught within a disciplinary (or even interdisciplinary) area, but the specific general education outcome is clearly stated and can later be assessed. If, for example, one of an institution's general education goals focuses on critical thinking, the specific outcome can be addressed in many types of courses and content areas.

With an outcomes-based general education program, faculty must all agree on what those outcomes will be. These discussions are difficult and time-consuming, but the results can be truly transformative. Some of the elements students gain through a general education course or sequence are more easily measured than others. Behaviors, skills, and content knowledge are relatively easily transformed into measurable outcomes. Other aspects of the goals of a general education program are more difficult to measure. How does one measure critical thinking? Certainly there are aspects that are measurable. It is possible, however, that other areas are; but when a faculty member states "I know it when I see it," there are measurable elements and a potential measurable outcome present. The difficulty is in getting to the heart of the goal in measurable ways.

General education programs that were created more than five years ago typically did not include outcomes for each area of the program. If there are not outcomes associated with a general education curriculum, measuring them becomes impossible. Unfortunately, many institutions have looked for measures for their general education program without first identifying the specific outcomes. So data can be found for many general education programs, but much of the data are not well connected to outcomes and are often therefore not used to improve teaching. If there are no specified and agreed upon outcomes, one of the first tasks is to create these outcomes. Clearly, not an easy job to undertake! It is, however, an essential step. When creating outcomes for an existing general education program or including construction of a revised general education plan, faculty engagement is crucial. Top-down approaches to implementing outcomes for general education rarely work. Instead, faculty-led work groups or committees should be used to identify the outcomes for each area of the curriculum.

Ensuring faculty collaboration for work with general education outcomes assessment and overall institutional effectiveness can be difficult. John Welsh and Jeff Metcalf (2003) describe an interview in which a faculty member stated, "I think most faculty see institutional effectiveness as a detraction from their jobs and a burden on them in terms of time and energy" (pp. 39–40). General education programs are certainly important and meaningful, but they will not be integrated and assessed in ways that lead to improvement until sufficient faculty support and leadership are in place. Integrating general education and its assessment is, by definition, a participatory process. Faculty must support and lead in developing the process, and in many cases they must assume the primary responsibility for planning the process and for using the resulting data.

Welsh and Metcalf identified three areas that were crucial if faculty were going to support institutional effectiveness efforts, including general education assessment. The first was that faculty need to view the primary motivation for the overall assessment process as focused on improvement of the institution rather than accountability to others: "The regression analysis demonstrates the point that institutional improvement is a more compelling justification for institutional effectiveness than is responsiveness to external mandates" (2003, p. 40). Second, they found that individual faculty are likely to be supportive of assessment efforts if they are directly involved with planning and following through on specific assessment activities. Finally, Welsh and Metcalf found that "outcomes oriented" faculty (those who defined "quality" as how well students were learning) were more supportive of assessment activities.

It is crucial to have both faculty support and faculty leadership as well. Steve Crowe, director of the Higher Learning Commission of the North Central Association, said in testimony before the national Commission in Accountability in Higher Education that "we have greatly underestimated faculty acceptance of accountability and, consequently, have not tapped their creativity in defining and implementing meaningful systems for it" (Crow, 2004, p. 3). Faculty collaboration in creating outcomes for general education is a step that cannot be overstated. Creation of outcomes and subsequent use of results will permit better integration of the overall general education program and for integration of the assessment results.

Most faculty are very good at measuring what students know, but it is often difficult for faculty to translate their skills in measuring student learning for a course to using that same knowledge to develop measurable outcomes for general education assessment. In a recent conversation with faculty from a particular department, one faculty member said that assessment would never work because it was too subjective. "Student learning in our area can't be measured" was his statement. However, it is clear that student learning can be measured, and actually was being measured regularly, because a quick review of the syllabus for one of his courses showed that he had exams, papers, and projects that all measured student learning. Even concepts that are difficult to measure precisely can be used in an assessment plan. General education outcomes are often very difficult to measure, so encouraging faculty dialogue on how to "best" measure the outcome can be a fruitful (if not frustrating) event. Likewise we can share the concept that assessing constructs such as critical thinking, ethical leadership, or communication skills does not have to be done in a "perfect way." As a matter of fact, it is likely that there is no perfect method for measuring these goals. However, there are ways to get closer to measuring the concept. As soon as a faculty members says "I know it when I see it," some type of measure can be identified. What is often the problem is not that a general education goal cannot be measured well; the issue is that faculty do not always agree on what the construct actually means. Ongoing dialogue and an open mind to hearing others can lead to some level of consensus.

Even after consensus is reached, however, writing the actual outcomes may prove difficult. Most faculty were never taught how to write an outcome that is measurable, so it is important that they be given the proper tools and information to do this well. Faculty members who have worked to create outcomes and are then told that the outcome is not written "correctly" or "in the proper form" do not tend to want to participate in other assessment activities. Therefore, it is important that faculty have access to workshops and staff members that can help them with their specific needs as they work on general education outcomes. Collaboration, trust, and good communication between the assessment leadership and faculty leading general education efforts are a vital part of a an integrated general education assessment paradigm.

Once general education assessment data are gathered, they must be used. On the surface, this seems a very simple step to take. However, it is quite astounding to see how much data exist on college campuses that are not actually used. There are drawers and files filled with papers and projects stored on the chance that an accreditor might one day want to see the data—but most never do. Data that result from general education assessment must get back into the hands of those faculty who are teaching in the general education program. At Texas Christian University, faculty learning communities (FLCs) were created for the interdisciplinary areas of their core curriculum. Assessment plans for each interdisciplinary area were created by the members of the FLC, and data collection is overseen by this group as well. Therefore, when results from the assessment are shared, they go back to the FLC members who are best situated to use the information to enhance and improve what they do in their core curriculum courses.

For the results of assessment plans to be used to improve and enhance teaching and learning, faculty need to feel confident that the data they collect will not be used against them. They must understand that the point of collecting assessment data about general education is to improve and enhance the overall program, not as summative evaluation data that could be used punitively. To make this a reality, deans and other decision makers must understand that the assessment process will work only if it is transparent, honest, and useful. The support given to faculty teaching general education is an important step in creating a culture that gathers, analyzes, and uses student learning data.

Professional Development and Scholarly Work

Several elements of the assessment of general education can be used for scholarly work. Knowing what and how much students are learning can lead to interesting research studies that focus on pedagogy, curriculum, or teaching innovations. This is true for disciplinary assessment work, but it is also true for assessment and scholarship in the area of general education. Several journals now have as a primary focus work on assessment or general education. Support for faculty who are using assessment data to inform their research is important and can gain large-scale faculty acceptance of the general education assessment process. Faculty may not see the results of their assessment process to be potential manuscripts, but with support from their institution it can be pointed out that the work they have done has value above and beyond the institution. The assessment office may be one of the few places on campus that sees the assessment work done across campus, and this can be an opportunity for the assessment office to encourage

NEW DIRECTIONS FOR TEACHING AND LEARNING • DOI: 10.1002/tl

a department or a specific faculty member to consider sharing his or her work. There are many regional and national higher education and assessment conferences. An institution can assist a faculty member's travel to one of these conferences because faculty who attend a nondisciplinary, higher education conference may be surprised by the range of sessions offered and the methods used by other institutions. Faculty often return from conferences as the biggest proponents of the assessment office and of developing meaningful and appropriate general education processes. After attending a conference on general education and assessment, one faculty member proudly announced she had just used the jargon "gen ed" in talking about general education. In the year following the conference, she led her department in developing creative measures for learning in economics and creating a senior capstone course.

Integrating General Education Assessment

Integration of general education into the overall educational curriculum for a baccalaureate degree is important. By following the history of the creation of general education, it becomes clear that how institutions view and use general education has and continues to be a work in progress. Assessing this curriculum has been a bit late in occurring, but it is necessary both for accountability accreditation and because using assessment results is one of the best ways to ensure ongoing enhancement of student learning. However, assessing general education is a difficult process, and few institutions are completely comfortable with their methods and uses of their data. Stanley Katz, director of the Center for Arts and Cultural Policy Studies at Princeton University, believes that most of the elements of general education are focused on thinking rather than content. He states that "what the liberal educator seeks to develop is the capacity to recognize meaningful problems and to identify the information and modes of analysis necessary to address them as well as the instinct to bring these to bear in problem solving. These capacities are much more difficult to measure" (2008, p. 33). These areas of general education are difficult to measure, but not impossible. The importance and usefulness of going through the process to create an integrated program make it well worth the time and effort.

Lessons Learned

In creating, implementing, and maintaining an assessable and integrated general education program, we can share several recommendations:

- Modifying any aspect of general education takes time. Trying to rush or push too hard to make changes usually results in little or no faculty engagement with the process or the results.

- Dialogue is almost always a good thing. Though there is certainly the possibility that talking takes so much time that little action ensues, encouraging all voices to be heard is an essential component of a transformative and integrated general education plan. Faculty, students, and even alumni often have strong opinions on what should be included in the program. Not everything will be developed into the final version, but making certain that nothing has been inadvertently left out can be checked.
- Make certain that the general education goals and outcomes are aligned with the overall mission of the institution.
- Gain consensus on measurable outcomes, and have them included in the statements regarding the general education plan. By doing this, you clarify the purpose of the general education programs for all constituents.
- Ensure that the methods for assessing the general education outcomes are useful for enhancing learning and for accountability. A lot of effort goes into collecting assessment data, and they should be used for the internal process of closing the loop and for demonstrating to others that the institution is effectively approaching assessment of general education.
- Plan for continued evaluation of the general education program and assessment strategies for that program. Using formative processes to regularly appraise the overall plan will allow "tweaking" modifications rather than a stagnant general education plan.

Integrating a general education program and its concomitant assessment plan enhances the probability that overall student learning will be regularly and meaningfully measured. This measurement will support informed decision making that may result in transformation of the institution.

References

Crow, S. (2004). *Testimony: The National Commission on Accountability in Higher Education*. Chicago, IL: The Higher Learning Commission of the North Central Association of Colleges and Schools. Retrieved on January 7, 2010, from http://www.sheeo.org/account/comm/testim/NCACS%20testimony.pdf.

Katz, S. N. (2008). Assessment and general education: Resisting reductionism without resisting responsibility. *Liberal Education, 94*(3), 30–37.

Marinara, M., Vajravelu, K., & Young, D. L. (2004). Making sense of the "loose baggy monster": Assessing learning in a general education program is a whale of a task. *Journal of General Education, 53*(1), 1–19.

Shulman, L. S. (2007). Counting and recounting: Assessment and the quest for accountability. *Change, 39*(1), 20–25.

Walvoord, B. E. (2004). *Assessment clear and simple: A practical guide for institutions, departments, and general education*. San Francisco, CA: Jossey-Bass.

Wehlburg, C. M. (2008). *Promoting integrated and transformative assessment: A deeper focus on student learning*. San Francisco: Jossey-Bass.

Wehlburg, C. M. (2010). Assessment practices in higher education. In K. Gillespie & D. Robertson (Eds.), A Guide to Faculty Development (2nd ed., pp. 242–261). San Francisco: Jossey-Bass.

Welsh, J. F., & Metcalf, J. (2003). Cultivating faculty support for institutional effectiveness activities: Benchmarking best practices. *Assessment and Evaluation in Higher Education, 28*, 33–45.

CATHERINE M. WEHLBURG *is the assistant provost for institutional effectiveness at Texas Christian University. She has taught psychology and educational psychology courses for more than a decade, serving as department chair for some of that time and then branching into faculty development and assessment. Wehlburg has worked with both the Higher Learning Commission of the North Central Association and the Commission on Colleges with the Southern Association of Colleges and Schools as an outside evaluator. She earned her Ph.D. in educational psychology from the University of Florida.*

INDEX

AAC&U. *See* Association of American Colleges and Universities

AASCU. *See* American Association of State Colleges and Universities

ABET Accredited Programs, 38

Adams, S., 9

Allen, M. J., 61

Alverno College, 42

American Association of State Colleges and Universities, 15, 16

Amherst University, 6

Anderegg, J., 24–25

APLU. *See* Association of Public Land-Grant Universities

Ash, S., 35

Ashville Institute on General Education (University of North Carolina), 71

Association of American Colleges and Universities (AAC&U), 7–9, 14, 16, 54, 60–61; Core Commitments Leadership Consortium, 53–55; and six types of general education curriculum, 60–61

Association of General and Liberal Studies, 79

Association of Public Land-Grant Universities (APLU), 15, 16

Atkinson, M. P., 44

Ballantine, T., 24–25

Barnett, R., 26

Bates College, 70–72, 76, 77; co-curricular learning at, 74–75; creating integrative general education at, 69–78; designing new general education curriculum at, 70–71; developmental learning at, 76–77; general education concentrations at, 73–74; general education curriculum at, 70–73; implementation of new curriculum at, 71–72; and integrated learning, 72–73

Berlin (Germany), 73

Bisesi, M., 4, 6

Blanchard, S., 37

Bloom's taxonomy, 42

Bok, D., 63

Boning, K., 4–8

Boyer, E. L., 4, 7

Bresciani, M., 37

Bush Foundation, 24

Byram, D., 24–25

CAAP. *See* Collegiate Assessment of Academic Proficiency

Carnegie Foundation for the Advancement of Teaching, 7, 75

Carnevale, T., 20

Carter, M., 37

Center for Arts and Cultural Policy Studies (Princeton University), 95

CLA. *See* Collegiate Learning Assessment

Co-curricular learning, 74–75

Cohen, A. M., 5

College Portrait (Web-reporting template), 15

Collegiate Assessment of Academic Proficiency (CAAP), 15–16

Collegiate Learning Assessment (CLA), 15–16

Columbia University, 6

Commission in Accountability in Higher Education, 93

Common intellectual experience curriculum, 61

Connected learning, 73–74

Core curriculum, 60; assessment and revision of, at Texas Christian University, 59–67

Crow, S., 93

Developmental learning, 76–77

Distribution model curriculum, 60

Elective system, 4, 7

Eliot, C., 4, 5

Emory University, 80, 85. *See also* Oxford College (Emory University)

Essential learning outcomes, 14. *See also* Outcomes, learning

Essential studies program, 30

Ferrandino, B., 59

Fink, K., 24–25

Fiore, S. R., 66

FIPSE. *See* Fund for the Improvement of Post Secondary Education

First Year Experience (FYE) programs, 9, 51, 55

Fund for the Improvement of Post Secondary Education (FIPSE), 15–16

Gaff, J. G., 4, 5, 7, 8
Galle, Jeffery, 79
Galle, Jo, 79
Gamson, Z. F., 26
Gano-Phillips, S., 26
General education: creating outcomes-based, 91–94; current issues in, 8–9; history of, 3–8; structure and strategies for, at University of North Dakota, 23–33
General education, assessment: and alignment of upper-level course and program outcomes with university and general education goals, 85–86; beginning process of building, 80–83; integrated and transformative, 89–96; integrating, 95; and professional development and scholarly work, 94–95; and sustained development, 83–85; three case studies in building integrated student learning outcomes-based, 79–87
General education, integrated: building integrated student learning outcomes assessment for, 79–87; creating (Bates College), 69–78; and current state of affairs, 8; lessons learned from creating, 95–96; and look back at general education, 3–8; as modern conceptualization of old idea, 10
"General Education in a Free Society" (Harvard University), 6
Georgetown Center on Education and the Workforce, 20
Great Books curriculum, 6
Greene, D. B., 38

Hanhan, S., 24–25
Hart, Peter D., Research Associates, 14
Harvard University, 4–6
Harward Center for Community Partnerships, 75
Hawthorne, J., 23
Head, J., 69
Heroic Mind (Vico), 66–67
Hewlett Foundation, 38, 41, 42
Hewlett Steering Committee, 36, 41
Higher Education Act (1965), 7
Higher Learning Commission, 79
Higher Learning Commission of the North Central Association, 93
Hyman, M., 38, 43

Inquiry-guided learning initiative (IGL; North Carolina State University), 32–33; faculty participation in, 37–39; further actions in, 39; lessons learned from, 43–45; major initiatives of, 40–41; overall findings from, 39–43; unifying undergraduate curriculum through, 35–46
Integrated learning, 72–73
Italy, 73

Jay, G., 9
Johns Hopkins University, 4

Kanter, S. L., 26
Katz, S. N., 95
Kelsch, A., 23
Kolb, D., 53
Kolb Learning Style Inventory, 53
Kuh, G., 18, 49, 56, 61

Latin America, 73
LEAP. See Liberal Education and America's Promise
Learning communities curriculum, 61
Lee, V. S., 35, 36, 42, 43
Levine, A., 4
Liberal Education and America's Promise (LEAP; AAC&U), 16
Liberal learning, 20–21
Lindblad, M., 42
London, H. B., 26
Lowell, A. L., 5
Luginbuhl, G., 38, 43

MAPP. See Measure of Academic Proficiency and Progress
Marinara, M., 90
Massachusetts Institute of Technology, 5–6
Matz, L., 47
McClure, A. L., 44
McNertney, E., 59, 65
Measure of Academic Proficiency and Progress (MAPP), 15–16
Meiklejohn, A., 6
Metcalf, J., 92–93
Miller, C., 15
Miller, G. E., 4
"Missions of the College Curriculum" (Carnegie Foundation), 7
Mississippi Delta, 73
Morrill-Land-Grant Act (1862), 5

NAICU. *See* National Association of Independent Colleges and Universities

National Association of Independent Colleges and Universities (NAICU), 15

National Research Council, 51

National Resource Center Conference on the First-Year Experience, 55

National Science Foundation, 45, 75; Research Experiences for Undergraduates (REU) internship, 75

National Survey of Student Engagement (NSSE), 15, 18–20, 85

Netherlands, 73

North Carolina State University, 35–46; Council on Undergraduate Education (CUE), 37, 38; Division of Undergraduate Affairs, 37; inquiry-guided learning (IGL) initiative, 35

NSSE. *See* National Survey of Student Engagement

Outcomes, learning: agreement on, 14–15; building assessment for integrated, 79–87; difficulties in achieving, 13–21; and efforts to report on and measure student learning, 15–16; and making learning excellence inclusive, 18–19; and VALUE project, 16–18

Oxford College (Emory University), 80–82, 85, 86

Pacific Seminars (PACS; University of the Pacific): assessment of student learning in, 53–54; campus collaboration in, 51–53; description of, 48–49; and faculty development, 53; and mean student self-ratings in 2007–2008 PACS 1 (all sections), 54*t*2; and mean student self-ratings in 2008–2009 PACS 2 (all sections), 55*t*3; and mean student self-ratings in 2008–2009 PACS 3 (all sections), 55*t*4; objectives and assignments, 50*t*1; origin of, 49–51; sustainability of, 54–56

PACS. *See* Pacific Seminars (PACS; University of the Pacific)

Paul, R., 37

Peter D. Hart Research Associates, 14

Preparation by Degrees survey (AASCU), 16

Priddy, L., 79, 87

Princeton University, 95

"Red Book," 6. *See also* "General Education in a Free Society" (Harvard University)

Reich, J., 69

Rhodes, T., 13

Riley, R., 21

SACS. *See* Southern Association for Colleges and Schools

Shoben, E., 7

Shulman, L. S., 90

Southern Association for Colleges and Schools (SACS), 82, 86

Southern Polytechnic State University (SPSU), 80, 82, 83, 85, 86

Spellings Commission, 15

SPSU. *See* Southern Polytechnic State University

Steen, T., 23

Stockton, California, 47

Student learning: efforts to report on and measure, 15–16; integrated, 19–20; and liberal learning on campus today, 20–21; making excellence in, inclusive, 18–19; and VALUE project, 16–18

TCU. *See* Texas Christian University

Texas Christian University (TCU), 59–67, 94; assessment and revision of core curriculum at, 64–66; core curriculum revision at, 59–67; course vetting process at, 63–64; design of core curriculum at, 61–63; emendation and course information policy at, 65–66; general education curriculum at, 60–64; implementing and managing core curriculum at, 64

Thematic required courses curriculum, 61

"Third era" (educational reform), 7

Thomas, R., 5

Tritelli, D., 21

U-CAN (Web-based template; NAICU), 15

UND. *See* University of North Dakota

Undergraduate curriculum, unifying, 35–46

University of Chicago, 6

University of Louisiana, Monroe, 80–86;

University Core Curriculum Committee (UCC), 80–83
University of North Carolina, 71
University of North Dakota, 23–33; Essential Studies Committee, 31; expanding understanding of general education at, 25–33; General Education Longitudinal Study (GELS), 24; General Education Requirements Committee (GERC), 25, 26; identifying program goals at, 26–29; implementing new requirements at, 29–30; initiating general education reform at, 26; lessons from essential studies program at, 30–32; and making general education matter more, 32–33; structures and strategies for general education at, 23–33; student attitudes about general education at, 24–25
University of the Pacific, 47–57; bookend seminars on good society at, 47–57; College of Arts and Sciences, 47, 48; university-wide objectives and outcomes of, 56–57. See also Pacific Seminars (PACS; University of the Pacific)
University of Wisconsin, 6
Upper-level requirements curriculum, 61
U.S. War Department, 5–6

Vajravelu, K., 90
Valid Assessment of Learning in Undergraduate Education (VALUE), 16–18
VALUE. See Valid Assessment of Learning in Undergraduate Education
Vico, G., 66–67
Vienna, 73
Voluntary System of Accountability (VSA), 15–16
VSA. See Voluntary System of Accountability

Wabash National Study of Liberal Arts Education, 19, 20, 85
Walvoord, B. E., 90
War Issues, 5–6
Washington Center, 61
Wehlburg, C. M., 1, 65, 89, 91
Wellman, J. D., 38
Welsh, J. F., 92–93
"What Are Learning Communities" (Washington Center), 61
Wills, J. B., 44
World War I, 5–6
World War II, 6

Young, D. L., 90

OTHER TITLES AVAILABLE IN THE
NEW DIRECTIONS FOR TEACHING AND LEARNING SERIES
Marilla D. Svinicki, Co-Editor-in-Chief
Catherine M. Wehlburg, Co-Editor-in-Chief
R. *Eugene Rice*, Consulting Editor

TL120 **As the Spirit Moves Us: Embracing Spirituality in the Postsecondary Experience**
Katherine Grace Hendrix, Janice D. Hamlet
During the past decade there has been an increased interest in how members of "first-world" countries cope with growing demands on their time, over-stimulation of the senses, increasing crime rates, and a generally hurried existence. Professors are hardly immune from these forces, and the results cascade onto students, communities, and ultimately, society in general. In contrast to the traditional Western forms of education, which address rational consensus whole eschewing the subjective, a holistic pedagogy suggests that engaging spirituality in one's classroom and profession is necessary for addressing concerns regarding human development and achievement. More specifically, scholars now espouse the value of holistic teaching—teaching that encompasses not only the mind but the soul as well. The contributors in this volume offer diverse vantage points from which to understand the impact of spirituality on well-being, its influence on classroom pedagogy and interpersonal relationships with students and colleagues, and its utility as a coping mechanism. The authors use auto-ethnography to capture the diversity of their perspectives and to display the power of the reflective voice.
ISBN: 978-04705-92632

TL119 **Designing Courses for Significant Learning: Voices of Experience**
L. Dee Fink, Arletta Knight Fink
Higher education today is being called on to deliver a new and more powerful kind of education, one that prepares students to be more engaged citizens, better equipped to solve complex problems at work and better prepared to lead meaningful lives individually. To respond to this call, teachers in colleges and universities need to learn how to design more powerful kinds of learning into their courses. In 2003, Dee Fink published a seminal book, *Creating Significant Learning Experiences*, that offered teachers two major tools for meeting this need: the Taxonomy of Significant Learning and the model of Integrated Course Design. Since that time, educators around the world have found Fink's ideas both visionary and inspiring. This issue of *New Directions for Teaching and Learning* contains multiple stories of how college-level teachers have used these ideas in a variety of teaching situations, with subject matter ranging from the sciences to the humanities. Their conclusion? The ideas in Fink's book truly make a difference. When used properly, they lead to major improvements in the level of student engagement and the quality of student learning!
ISBN: 978-04705-54807

TL118 **Internationalizing the Curriculum in Higher Education**
Carolin Kreber
Internationalization is a looming policy issue in higher education—yet precisely what it can add to the student learning experience and what it means with regard to teaching and learning are far too infrequently discussed or written about. This volume explores different meanings and rationales underlying the notion of internationalization in higher education. Although internationalization efforts in higher education have become increasingly

driven by economic considerations, finance is not an appropriate foundation for all initiatives, particularly those at the level of curriculum, where academic, social/cultural, ethical, political and even environmental rationales feature more strongly. The chapter authors provide a rich conceptual basis from which to appreciate concrete efforts directed at internationalizing curricula, and they describe nine cases of internationalization initiatives at the curricular level. The volume further suggests that consideration of internationalization in higher education must look both within specific programs and across programs. It cannot be separated from fundamental questions about the purposes of higher education and the roles of teachers, students, administrators, and the institution as a whole in fulfilling those purposes. ISBN: 978-04705-37350

TL117   **Improving the Climate for Undergraduate Teaching and Learning in STEM Fields**
Roger G. Baldwin
The quality of undergraduate education in science, technology, engineering, and mathematics (STEM) fields has been a national concern since the time of Sputnik. In spite of many reports on the state of STEM undergraduate education and multiple reform efforts, time-worn patterns of instruction persist in many STEM classrooms and laboratories. It is increasingly clear that major improvements to STEM under-graduate education require the interest and active engagement of key stakeholders, including STEM instructors, academic administrators, disciplinary societies, and government policy-makers. This volume looks at the challenges of enhancing STEM education from the perspective of these different stakeholders. Each chapter provides an illumi-nating analysis of problems facing STEM education and suggests actions needed to strengthen STEM undergraduate education in a time when science and technology competence are more important than ever. The strategies advanced in this volume should be key elements of the coordinated, systemic effort necessary to implement lasting reform of STEM undergraduate education.
ISBN: 978-04704-97289

TL116   **Team-Based Learning: Small-Group Learning's Next Big Step**
Larry K. Michaelsen, Michael Sweet, Dean X. Parmelee
Team-Based Learning (TBL) is a unique form of small-group learning designed in and for the college classroom. TBL's special combination of incentives and corrective feedback quickly transforms groups into high-performance learning teams, with no time taken from the coverage of course content. In this issue of *New Directions for Teaching and Learning*, the authors describe the practical elements of TBL, how it can look in the classroom, and what they have learned as it has grown into an inter-disciplinary and international practice. Importantly, TBL is not about teaching but about learning. Several articles in this volume illustrate this emphasis by using TBL students' own words to reinforce key ideas.
ISBN: 978-04704-62126

TL115   **The Role of the Classroom in College Student Persistence**
John M. Braxton
This issue of *New Directions for Teaching and Learning* brings into sharp focus the complex role college and university faculty play in shaping the persistence and departure decisions of undergraduate students. The authors review practices ranging from curricular structures and instructional staffing policies to faculty teaching methods, and they offer recommendations for many common problems. Taken together, the chapters outline the elements of a scholarship of practice centered on keeping students in school. College and university presidents, chief academic affairs officers, academic deans, directors and staff members of campus-based centers for teaching, and

individuals responsible for enrollment management will find a great deal of practical wisdom in this volume.
ISBN: 978-04704-22168

TL114   Information Literacy: One Key to Education
Margit Misangyi Watts
This issue draws on the expertise of librarians and faculty to highlight the central role of information literacy in higher education. The authors show how approaches to information literacy can be used to engage undergraduates in research and creative scholarship. The articles clarify definitions of information literacy and illustrate various means of curricular integration. Students regularly miss the relationship between the information-seeking process and the actual creation of knowledge. The authors in this issue support infusing the undergraduate curriculum with research-based learning to facilitate students' ability to define research for themselves. Most importantly, this volume argues, students' information literacy leads beyond finding information—it actually involves their creating knowledge. Education should focus on inquiry, research, and discovery as a frame of mind. Our goal as educators should be to maintain and strengthen the *context* of learning while enhancing the *content* of a liberal education. This finally rests—as it always has—on a foundation of incorporating information literacy skills. Recent dramatic changes in the meaning of "information literacy" have left many educators scrambling to keep up. What has not changed is the importance of teaching students to find information that matters and then helping them figure out *why* it matters. These chapters can help us all integrate the new world of digital information into a relevant, timely approach to content and teaching practice.
ISBN: 978-04703-98715

TL113   Educating Integrated Professionals: Theory and Practice on Preparation for the Professoriate
Carol L. Colbeck, KerryAnn O'Meara, Ann E. Austin
This volume explores how to enhance doctoral education by preparing future faculty to integrate their work in two interrelated ways. The first mode encourages doctoral students—and their faculty mentors—to take advantage of the synergies among their teaching, research, and community service roles. The second mode of integration emphasizes connections between professional and academic aspects of faculty work. The authors draw on theories of identity development, professionalization, apprenticeship, socialization, mentoring, social networks, situated curriculum, concurrent curricula, and academic planning to illuminate some of the drawbacks of current education for the professoriate. They also point toward current programs and new possibilities for educating doctoral students who will be ready to begin their faculty careers as professionals who integrate teaching, research, and service.
ISBN: 978-04702-95403

TL112   Curriculum Development in Higher Education: Faculty-Driven Processes and Practices
Peter Wolf, Julia Christensen Hughes
Faculty within institutions of higher education are increasingly being asked to play leadership roles in curriculum assessment and reform initiatives. This change is being driven by quality concerns; burgeoning disciplinary knowledge; interest in a broader array of learning outcomes, including skills and values; and growing support for constructivist pedagogies and learning-centered, interdisciplinary curricula. It is essential that faculty be well prepared to take a scholarly approach to this work. To that end, this issue of *New Directions for Teaching and Learning* presents the frameworks used and lessons learned by faculty, administrators, and educational developers in a variety of

curriculum assessment and development processes. Collectively, the authors in this volume present the context and catalysts of higher education curriculum reform, advocate for the Scholarship of Curriculum Practice (SoCP), provide examples of curricular assessment and development initiatives at a variety of institutional levels, suggest that educational developers can provide much support to such processes, and argue that this work has profound implications for the faculty role. Anyone involved in curriculum assessment and development will find food for thought in each chapter.
ISBN: 978-04702-78512

TL111   Scholarship of Multicultural Teaching and Learning
Matthew Kaplan, A.T. Miller
Because effective approaches to multicultural teaching and learning are still being developed in institutions across the U.S. and around the world, it is essential to study and document promising practices. It is only through rigorous research and comparative studies that we can be assured that the significant investments many institutions are making in multicultural education for the development of individual student and faculty skills, and the overall betterment of society, will reap positive results. This volume of *New Directions for Teaching and Learning* provides the valuable results of such research as well as models for the types of research that others could carry out in this area. The volume will appeal to new and experienced practitioners of multicultural teaching. It offers documented illustrations of how such teaching is designed, carried out, and is effective in varied higher education contexts and in a wide range of disciplines representing the humanities, social sciences, engineering and math, and the arts.
ISBN: 978-04702-23826

TL110   Neither White Nor Male: Female Faculty of Color
Katherine Grace Hendrix
Given limited information on the academic experience in general and on the pedagogical strategies and strengths of faculty of color in particular, the scholars in this issue have come together to begin the process of articulating the academic experiences of female professors of color. While chronicling our challenges within academia as well as our contributions to the education of U.S. students, this collaborative effort will add depth to the existing literature on faculty of color, serve as a reference for positioning women of color within the larger context of higher education (moving us from the margin to the center), and lay a foundation for more inclusive future research.
ISBN: 04702-2382-6

TL109   Self-Authorship: Advancing Students' Intellectual Growth
Peggy S. Meszaros
This issue addresses the limitations of national efforts to focus students' intellectual development narrowly on testing and explores why educators in higher education should consider using the lens of self-authorship and the Learning Partnerships Model for a more holistic model of student intellectual development. The chapters provide examples of institutional transformations needed to support change in teaching and learning and examples of assessment, research, and curricular development based in self-authorship theory. The summary chapter by Marcia Baxter Magolda ties the themes from each of the chapters together and offers promise for the future. The final chapter provides ideas for next steps in promoting the use of self-authorship to advance the intellectual development of college students. The audience for this volume is broad, ranging from college faculty to student affairs faculty and staff to college administrators who are facing assessment

challenges for reporting student learning outcomes to their various constituencies, agencies, and boards. This volume should also prove instructive to
faculty embarking on curriculum revisions and identifying and measuring
student learning outcomes for undergraduate and graduate students.
ISBN: 07879-9721-2

TL108 **Developing Student Expertise and Community: Lessons from How People
Learn**
Anthony J. Petrosino, Taylor Martin, Vanessa Svihla
This issue presents research from a collaboration among learning scientists,
assessment experts, technologists, and subject-matter experts, with the goal
of producing adaptive expertise in students. The model is based on the
National Research Council book *How People Learn*. The chapters present
case studies of working together to develop learning environments centered
on challenge-based instruction. While the strategies and research come from
engineering, they are applicable across disciplines to help students think
about the process of problem solving.
ISBN: 07879-9574-6

TL107 **Exploring Research-Based Teaching**
Carolin Kreber
Investigates the wide scope research-based teaching, while focusing on two
distinct forms. The first sees research-based teaching as student-focused,
inquiry-based learning; students become generators of knowledge. The
second perspective fixes the lens on teachers; the teaching is characterized
by discipline-specific inquiry into the teaching process itself. Both methods
have positive effects on student learning, and this volume explores research
and case studies.
ISBN: 07879-9077-9

TL106 **Supplemental Instruction: New Visions for Empowering Student Learning**
Marion E. Stone, Glen Jacobs
Supplemental Instruction (SI) is an academic support model introduced over
thirty years ago to help students be successful in difficult courses. SI teaches
students how to learn via regularly scheduled, out-of-class collaborative
sessions with other students. This volume both introduces the tenets of SI to
beginners and brings those familiar up to speed with today's methods and
the future directions. Includes case studies, how-to's, benefits to students
and faculty, and more.
ISBN: 0-7879-8680-1

TL105 **A Laboratory for Public Scholarship and Democracy**
Rosa A. Eberly, Jeremy Cohen
Public scholarship has grown out of the scholarship-and-service model, but
its end is democracy rather than volunteerism. The academy has intellectual
and creative resources that can help build involved, democratic communities
through public scholarship. Chapters present concepts, processes, and case
studies from Penn State's experience with public scholarship.
ISBN: 0-7879-8530-9

TL104 **Spirituality in Higher Education**
Sherry L. Hoppe, Bruce W. Speck
With chapters by faculty and administrators, this book investigates the role
of spirituality in educating the whole student while recognizing that how
spirituality is viewed, taught, and experienced is intensely personal. The goal
is not to prescribe a method for integrating spirituality but to offer options

and perspectives. Readers will be reminded that the quest for truth and meaning, not the destination, is what is vitally important.
ISBN: 0-7879-8363-2

TL103   Identity, Learning, and the Liberal Arts
Ned Scott Laff
Argues that we must foster conversations between liberal studies and student development theory, because the skills inherent in liberal learning are the same skills used for personal development. Students need to experience core learning that truly influences their critical thinking skills, character development, and ethics. Educators need to design student learning encounters that develop these areas. This volume gives examples of how liberal arts education can be a healthy foundation for life skills.
ISBN: 0-7879-8333-0

TL102   Advancing Faculty Learning Through Interdisciplinary Collaboration
Elizabeth G. Creamer, Lisa R. Lattuca
Explores why stakeholders in higher education should refocus attention on collaboration as a form of faculty learning. Chapters give theoretical basis then practical case studies for collaboration's benefits in outreach, scholarship, and teaching. Also discusses impacts on education policy, faculty hiring and development, and assessment of collaborative work.
ISBN: 0-7879-8070-6

TL101   Enhancing Learning with Laptops in the Classroom
Linda B. Nilson, Barbara E. Weaver
This volume contains case studies—mostly from Clemson University's leading-edge laptop program—that address victories as well as glitches in teaching with laptop computers in the classroom. Disciplines using laptops include psychology, music, statistics, animal sciences, and humanities. The volume also advises faculty on making a laptop mandate successful at their university, with practical guidance for both pedagogy and student learning.
ISBN: 0-7879-8049-8

TL100   Alternative Strategies for Evaluating Student Learning
Michelle V. Achacoso, Marilla D. Svinicki
Teaching methods are adapting to the modern era, but innovation in assessment of student learning lags behind. This volume examines theory and practical examples of creative new methods of evaluation, including authentic testing, testing with multimedia, portfolios, group exams, visual synthesis, and performance-based testing. Also investigates improving students' ability to take and learn from tests, before and after.
ISBN: 0-7879-7970-8

TL99   Addressing Faculty and Student Classroom Improprieties
John M. Braxton, Alan E. Bayer
Covers the results of a large research study on occurrence and perceptions of classroom improprieties by both students and faculty. When classroom norms are violated, all parties in a classroom are affected, and teaching and learning suffer. The authors offer guidelines for both student and faculty classroom behavior and how institutions might implement those suggestions.
ISBN: 0-7879-7794-2

TL98   Decoding the Disciplines: Helping Students Learn Disciplinary Ways of Thinking
David Pace, Joan Middendorf
The Decoding the Disciplines model is a way to teach students the critical-thinking skills required to understand their specific discipline. Faculty define

bottlenecks to learning, dissect the ways experts deal with the problematic issues, and invent ways to model experts' thinking for students. Chapters are written by faculty in diverse fields who successfully used these methods and became involved in the scholarship of teaching and learning.
ISBN: 0-7879-7789-6

TL97 **Building Faculty Learning Communities**
Milton D. Cox, Laurie Richlin
A very effective way to address institutional challenges is a faculty learning community. FLCs are useful for preparing future faculty, reinvigorating senior faculty, and implementing new courses, curricula, or campus initiatives. The results of FLCs parallel those of student learning communities, such as retention, deeper learning, respect for others, and greater civic participation. This volume describes FLCs from a practitioner's perspective, with plenty of advice, wisdom, and lessons for starting your own FLC.
ISBN: 0-7879-7568-0

TL96 **Online Student Ratings of Instruction**
Trav D. Johnson, D. Lynn Sorenson
Many institutions are adopting Web-based student ratings of instruction, or are considering doing it, because online systems have the potential to save time and money among other benefits. But they also present a number of challenges. The authors of this volume have firsthand experience with electronic ratings of instruction. They identify the advantages, consider costs and benefits, explain their solutions, and provide recommendations on how to facilitate online ratings.
ISBN: 0-7879-7262-2

TL95 **Problem-Based Learning in the Information Age**
Dave S. Knowlton, David C. Sharp
Provides information about theories and practices associated with problem-based learning, a pedagogy that allows students to become more engaged in their own education by actively interpreting information. Today's professors are adopting problem-based learning across all disciplines to faciliate a broader, modern definition of what it means to learn. Authors provide practical experience about designing useful problems, creating conducive learning environments, facilitating students' activities, and assessing students' efforts at problem solving.
ISBN: 0-7879-7172-3

TL94 **Technology: Taking the Distance out of Learning**
Margit Misangyi Watts
This volume addresses the possibilities and challenges of computer technology in higher education. The contributors examine the pressures to use technology, the reasons not to, the benefits of it, the feeling of being a learner as well as a teacher, the role of distance education, and the place of computers in the modern world. Rather than discussing only specific successes or failures, this issue addresses computers as a new cultural symbol and begins meaningful conversations about technology in general and how it affects education in particular.
ISBN: 0-7879-6989-3

TL93 **Valuing and Supporting Undergraduate Research**
Joyce Kinkead
The authors gathered in this volume share a deep belief in the value of undergraduate research. Research helps students develop skills in problem solving, critical thinking, and communication, and undergraduate researchers' work can contribute to an institution's quest to further knowledge and help meet societal challenges. Chapters provide an overview

of undergraduate research, explore programs at different types of institutions, and offer suggestions on how faculty members can find ways to work with undergraduate researchers.
ISBN: 0-7879-6907-9

TL92   **The Importance of Physical Space in Creating Supportive Learning Environments**
Nancy Van Note Chism, Deborah J. Bickford
The lack of extensive dialogue on the importance of learning spaces in higher education environments prompted the essays in this volume. Chapter authors look at the topic of learning spaces from a variety of perspectives, elaborating on the relationship between physical space and learning, arguing for an expanded notion of the concept of learning spaces and furnishings, talking about the context within which decision making for learning spaces takes place, and discussing promising approaches to the renovation of old learning spaces and the construction of new ones.
ISBN: 0-7879-6344-5

TL91   **Assessment Strategies for the On-Line Class: From Theory to Practice**
Rebecca S. Anderson, John F. Bauer, Bruce W. Speck
Addresses the kinds of questions that instructors need to ask themselves as they begin to move at least part of their students' work to an on-line format. Presents an initial overview of the need for evaluating students' on-line work with the same care that instructors give to the work in hard-copy format. Helps guide instructors who are considering using on-line learning in conjunction with their regular classes, as well as those interested in going totally on-line.
ISBN: 0-7879-6343-7

TL90   **Scholarship in the Postmodern Era: New Venues, New Values, New Visions**
Kenneth J. Zahorski
A little over a decade ago, Ernest Boyer's *Scholarship Reconsidered* burst upon the academic scene, igniting a robust national conversation that maintains its vitality to this day. This volume aims at advancing that important conversation. Its first section focuses on the new settings and circumstances in which the act of scholarship is being played out; its second identifies and explores the fresh set of values currently informing today's scholarly practices; and its third looks to the future of scholarship, identifying trends, causative factors, and potentialities that promise to shape scholars and their scholarship in the new millennium.
ISBN: 0-7879-6293-7

TL89   **Applying the Science of Learning to University Teaching and Beyond**
Diane F. Halpern, Milton D. Hakel
Seeks to build on empirically validated learning activities to enhance what and how much is learned and how well and how long it is remembered. Demonstrates that the movement for a real science of learning—the application of scientific principles to the study of learning—has taken hold both under the controlled conditions of the laboratory and in the messy real-world settings where most of us go about the business of teaching and learning.
ISBN: 0-7879-5791-7

TL88   **Fresh Approaches to the Evaluation of Teaching**
Christopher Knapper, Patricia Cranton
Describes a number of alternative approaches, including interpretive and critical evaluation, use of teaching portfolios and teaching awards,

performance indicators and learning outcomes, technology-mediated evaluation systems, and the role of teacher accreditation and teaching scholarship in instructional evaluation.
ISBN: 0-7879-5789-5

TL87   **Techniques and Strategies for Interpreting Student Evaluations**
Karron G. Lewis
Focuses on all phases of the student rating process—from data-gathering methods to presentation of results. Topics include methods of encouraging meaningful evaluations, mid-semester feedback, uses of quality teams and focus groups, and creating questions that target individual faculty needs and interest.
ISBN: 0-7879-5789-5

TL86   **Scholarship Revisited: Perspectives on the Scholarship of Teaching**
Carolin Kreber
Presents the outcomes of a Delphi Study conducted by an international panel of academics working in faculty evaluation scholarship and postsecondary teaching and learning. Identifies the important components of scholarship of teaching, defines its characteristics and outcomes, and explores its most pressing issues.
ISBN: 0-7879-5447-0

TL85   **Beyond Teaching to Mentoring**
Alice G. Reinarz, Eric R. White
Offers guidelines to optimizing student learning through classroom activities as well as peer, faculty, and professional mentoring. Addresses mentoring techniques in technical training, undergraduate business, science, and liberal arts studies, health professions, international study, and interdisciplinary work.
ISBN: 0-7879-5617-1

NEW DIRECTIONS FOR TEACHING AND LEARNING
ORDER FORM SUBSCRIPTION AND SINGLE ISSUES

DISCOUNTED BACK ISSUES:

Use this form to receive 20% off all back issues of *New Directions for Teaching and Learning.*
All single issues priced at **$23.20** (normally $29.00)

TITLE	ISSUE NO.	ISBN
_____	_____	_____
_____	_____	_____
_____	_____	_____

Call 888-378-2537 or see mailing instructions below. When calling, mention the promotional code JBXND to receive your discount. For a complete list of issues, please visit www.josseybass.com/go/ndtl

SUBSCRIPTIONS: (1 YEAR, 4 ISSUES)

☐ New Order   ☐ Renewal

U.S.	☐ Individual: $89	☐ Institutional: $242
CANADA/MEXICO	☐ Individual: $89	☐ Institutional: $282
ALL OTHERS	☐ Individual: $113	☐ Institutional: $316

Call 888-378-2537 or see mailing and pricing instructions below.
Online subscriptions are available at www.interscience.wiley.com

ORDER TOTALS:

Issue / Subscription Amount: $ _____

Shipping Amount: $ _____
(for single issues only – subscription prices include shipping)

Total Amount: $ _____

SHIPPING CHARGES:		
SURFACE	**DOMESTIC**	**CANADIAN**
First Item	$5.00	$6.00
Each Add'l Item	$3.00	$1.50

(No sales tax for U.S. subscriptions. Canadian residents, add GST for subscription orders. Individual rate subscriptions must be paid by personal check or credit card. Individual rate subscriptions may not be resold as library copies.)

BILLING & SHIPPING INFORMATION:

☐ **PAYMENT ENCLOSED:** *(U.S. check or money order only. All payments must be in U.S. dollars.)*

☐ **CREDIT CARD:**   ☐ VISA   ☐ MC   ☐ AMEX

Card number _____ Exp. Date_____

Card Holder Name_____ Card Issue # *(required)* _____

Signature _____ Day Phone_____

☐ **BILL ME:** *(U.S. institutional orders only. Purchase order required.)*

Purchase order # _____
Federal Tax ID 13559302 • GST 89102-8052

Name_____

Address_____

Phone_____ E-mail_____

Copy or detach page and send to: **John Wiley & Sons, PTSC, 5th Floor**
989 Market Street, San Francisco, CA 94103-1741

Order Form can also be faxed to: **888-481-2665**

PROMO JBXND

NEW DIRECTIONS FOR TEACHING AND LEARNING IS NOW AVAILABLE ONLINE AT WILEY INTERSCIENCE

What is Wiley InterScience?

Wiley InterScience is the dynamic online content service from John Wiley & Sons delivering the full text of over 300 leading scientific, technical, medical, and professional journals, plus major reference works, the acclaimed Current Protocols laboratory manuals, and even the full text of select Wiley print books online.

What are some special features of Wiley InterScience?

Wiley Interscience Alerts is a service that delivers table of contents via e-mail for any journal available on Wiley InterScience as soon as a new issue is published online.
EarlyView is Wiley's exclusive service presenting individual articles online as soon as they are ready, even before the release of the compiled print issue. These articles are complete, peer-reviewed, and citable.
CrossRef is the innovative multi-publisher reference linking system enabling readers to move seamlessly from a reference in a journal article to the cited publication, typically located on a different server and published by a different publisher.

How can I access Wiley InterScience?

Visit http://www.interscience.wiley.com.

Guest Users can browse Wiley InterScience for unrestricted access to journal tables of contents and article abstracts, or use the powerful search engine.
Registered Users are provided with a *Personal Home Page* to store and manage customized alerts, searches, and links to favorite journals and articles. Additionally, Registered Users can view free online sample issues and preview selected material from major reference works.
Licensed Customers are entitled to access full-text journal articles in PDF, with select journals also offering full-text HTML.

How do I become an Authorized User?

Authorized Users are individuals authorized by a paying Customer to have access to the journals in Wiley InterScience. For example, a university that subscribes to Wiley journals is considered to be the Customer. Faculty, staff, and students authorized by the university to have access to those journals in Wiley InterScience are Authorized Users. Users should contact their library for information on which Wiley journals they have access to in Wiley InterScience.

ASK YOUR INSTITUTION ABOUT WILEY INTERSCIENCE TODAY!